I BELIEVE and YOU Can Too

KIERAN BANKS

AMBASSADOR INTERNATIONAL
GREENVILLE, SOUTH CAROLINA & BELFAST, NORTHERN IRELAND

www.ambassador-international.com

I Believe and You Can Too

Paperback: ISBN: 978-1-64960-199-5

Printed in UK

Ambassador International
Emerald House
411 University Ridge, Suite B14
Greenville, SC 29601
www.ambassador-international.com

Ambassador Books and Media
The Mount
2 Woodstock Link
Belfast, BT6 8DD, Northern Ireland, UK
www.ambassadormedia.co.uk

To Sheena, my wife,
whose love and encouragement
brought this little book to life.

Philippians 1v3

Contents

1   The Pages of our Lives   7

2   Reasons to Believe   15

3   The One who got it Right   23

4   The Heart of the Matter   35

5   The Good News   45

6   The Signs of Life   53

7   The Family of the Firstborn   61

8   Our Future Hope   73

9   The Invitation   85

     References   91

1

The Pages of our Lives

Life at home began for me in 1959 in a labourer's cottage, in Northern Ireland. My Grandmother, mother, and I lived here until I was about two years old. It had none of the mod-cons we associate with modern living, and I'm not talking microwave ovens. This house had no running water. Each day would therefore begin with a trip to a fast-flowing stream a few hundred yards away, where two buckets were filled to service our needs for the day.

My father's family lived in the same village. Home for them was a log cabin where my paternal grandmother had to walk further, but to a pump, for her water. Of course, water wasn't all they drank. Grandfather kept a cow that grazed in a field a good half-mile from the house. After a little encouragement, she would walk the distance home by herself to be milked, then return to the field where the obliging neighbour who had first opened the gate, now closed it behind her. When I look around me today, at the gadgets I take for granted, and the goods we acquire each week, off packed supermarket shelves, the times have certainly changed.

By my early primary school years, the family had moved into the big city. One of my earliest memories, growing up in a Belfast street of the 1960s, is of being made to attend a mission hall Sunday school. Unfortunately, rather than inspire, it became the scene of great personal embarrassment for me. One Sunday I decided to bunk off and play with a friend two streets away. To my great surprise, mother and father had decided to go for a stroll that Sunday morning, and in doing so discovered their erring son. Father wasn't a man to be trifled with or easily inclined to forgive. I was dragged by the scruff of the neck to the hall, its door swung open, and myself thrown unceremoniously into the middle of the hushed gathering. Although I don't recall my father ever attending any church himself, he felt my need was greater than his, and he may have been right.

Growing up into my teens was peppered with the usual miscreant behaviour of many boys my age. The one source of danger I was spared was the political and paramilitary scene. The early 1970s were among the worst years for this kind of activity with kneecapping, bus burnings and much worse. I recall one night being elected by 'friends' to go to the local off-license and was spotted and chased by a gang of older boys. I was caught and questioned to find out which side of the political divide I lived on. When I told them I went to the same Protestant school most of them did, it looked like I might live to see another day. Unfortunately, upon release, one of the gang asked my name, to which I foolishly replied, "Ciaran" an unmistakably Catholic name, reflecting my very earliest up-bringing. I was beaten up, "just to be on the safe side," they told me.

At the age of sixteen, and with the prospect of adult working life ahead of me, I was eager to hear of a planned visit to our school by a Royal Naval careers officer. I listened with wrapped attention as he spoke of the opportunities the various branches offered, the countries one would visit, the life-long friends one would make. I was impressed. But when he told me I could join in the Easter, thus avoiding scheduled summer term exams, I was smitten. I went to Belfast, sat my entrance exam, and took the Queen's Shilling. Before I knew it, the day of departure had arrived. I stood on the jetty hugging and kissing family members. "I'll be fine," I assured them all and strode confidently aboard the Belfast-Liverpool ferry.

So began a whole new chapter of life. The two years boy's time and three years man's time, inducted me into real if not 'responsible' adult life. The cost of freedom from the restraints of home came quickly though; too quickly. The first night on the ferry saw me befriended by another sailor returning from leave. He suggested a few drinks together and not wishing to appear less the man, I agreed. After three pints of heavy, I was heaving - over the side of the boat, and that to the early hours! It soon became apparent, with naval training behind me, and life on board ahead of me, that alcohol would feature significantly in life as a sailor. Whether it was ashore in Portsmouth or Plymouth, around the Mediterranean or the Caribbean, the goal was always to find watering holes. Whilst not all our pursuits were as noble as they might have been, I did learn the value of true friendship and the heightened value of any experience that can be shared.

My first ship was an aircraft carrier. When I joined it, HMS Ark Royal had already made a name for itself on national television, and its theme tune a chart-topping success, courtesy of Rod Stewart. By the time I arrived the BBC wanted to re-release the hit, sung this time by the ship's company. We all duly assembled on the flight deck and sang our little hearts out into a hovering, very fluffy, microphone. For the benefit of music aficionados, the 'B' side was 'Remember you're a Womble.' Sometime later the BBC requested that three sailors appear on Top of the Pops to accompany the song as Pan's People danced to it. Incredibly, yours truly was one of those chosen. I was ordered to freshen up my No.1's, and report to the duty officer. Apparently, a taxi was being sent to collect us. However, at the very last minute, and to my

profound disappointment, the feature was dropped in favour
of some other song. The record was rereleased to the great
enjoyment of at least one fan, my mother, who held on to it
up until she died.

Several aspects of life on board were blessings. You lived
cheek by jowl with one another. 'Getting on' wasn't desirable,
it was essential. You learned to accommodate each other or
tried to. Occasionally, you wondered if your own individuality
hadn't jumped ship, or sunk without trace. After all, everyone
dressed the same, often spoke the same, behaved the same,
slept in the same space, ate the same food, and played the
same. Finding who one was, oneself, in all this 'sameness'
could be hard. I recall vividly one Chief Petty Officer in charge
of outside machinery who decorated his workspace with
texts from the bible. Although we sniggered at his oddity, I
was secretly impressed that at least in one man's experience
something was worth walking the other way for.

As it happens, a few years later, a whole new set of
coordinates were plotted on my horizon. Sometime in 1980,
after a drinking session ashore in Plymouth with friends, I
decided to walk the few miles back to the ship, alone. I called
into a small hotel for a snack and got talking to a young man
who spoke of Jesus Christ. I wasted no time telling him he
was wasting his. I had grown up where religion, it seemed to
me, had divided a community; he was talking to the wrong
man! Before appearing to leave, he asked: "If there was a God
would you want to meet him?" Although I sensed something
of a trap, this seemed a dangerous question to hear oneself
say "no" to. He wanted to pray for me, and I nervously
agreed. As he prayed, I was moved by his sincere desire that
the Lord speak into my life. When he stopped, I felt utterly
overwhelmed by what I can only call a sense of encounter. All
I recall repeating several times was the word "sorry," which I
confess felt more drawn from me than spoken by me.

I could no more explain what had happened to me that night than fly to the moon, but something had. I left the hotel, lit up another cigarette, and resolved not to share any of what had happened with anyone. It would almost certainly destroy what little credibility I had with those who knew me.

Eventually, with my time served, I left the Navy. I was discharged in 1980 from HMS Nelson, Portsmouth. I decided to rent a bedsit in the city. It was during this time that I bought a copy of the Bible and also set out on evenings to find a church where there may be those who could help me grasp better what had happened to me that night in Plymouth. The first church I came to told me they were 'full.' I've since felt they must have been referring to their youth club, as not long after, I visited on a Sunday and attendance was sparse. On a second trip out I discovered a church where, I'm pleased to say, I was received warmly and supported much by one particular elder.

Civvy street takes some getting used to after life in any of the 'services,' but get used to it I had to. I was married and became the proud father of two wonderful daughters. Working life included, oh so briefly, becoming an insurance salesman; then a precision lathe setter for an optical company; a painter-decorator's mate; then after graduating, a teacher, and eventually headteacher; and now finally, a Baptist Minister. As I reflect on these employments, I'm often conscious that varied though they be, each contributed something to make the next step possible. Each was its distinctive chapter, but still belonging to the same book.

In Shakespeare's most famous play, Hamlet tells Horatio, "there's a divinity that shapes our ends. Rough hew them how he will." The reference seems to be to that irrepressible sense in life that our own choices are not all that shape our destiny. They often set in motion such a chain of unanticipated outcomes; new places we find ourselves, new people we come to know and new opportunities we never imagined. This is a simple recognition that much of what we experience in life is 'given' rather than determined by us. And for me, a seemingly random encounter that night with a young man falls into this category. It was an event that had something of felt appointment about it.

In one conversation with a religious professional (John 3v1-16), Jesus says the activity of God in life is like the wind that blows wherever it pleases. You hear its sound, but you cannot tell where it comes from or where it is going. In a world of both earthly and spiritual things, Jesus challenges the man, and us all, to recognise the difference.

The invitation is to stand back and read the particular book that is our lives. Its surface details will be only too apparent; where new chapters begin, and old one's end. Where new characters appear, and others leave. Where dark clouds hover, but also the times of resolution where some of those clouds prove to have silver linings. All these are the surface detail in every life, but God, having placed eternity in human hearts (Ecclesiastes 3v11) is calling us to far, far more than playing with surface detail. When we find ourselves thinking 'there must be more to life than this' often the Spirit of God is breathing into our lives an air of divine discontentment with all that is less than himself.

Maybe we, ourselves, have come to this point in our own lives. One reaction might be to shrug it off or fill the space with some distraction. Alternatively, we might ask if God is seeking to break through into our lives. According to the NT (Luke 15), he is always at work doing this very thing, searching out what has become lost - and he is very good at it. Just a week before writing this, I was a guest speaker at a church in a small Scottish hillside town and shared my testimony of forty years before, and five hundred miles distant. After the service, a middle-aged man came to speak to me, and described the same small hotel I had spoken of, where he too had met the same young man, heard the same message, and come to know the same God. He, it seems, 'does not live in temples built by human hands,' but dwells in the 'givens' of life, 'so that we might seek him and perhaps reach out for him, though he is not far from any one of us.'

So, we might ask again, "where am I in the book that is my life?" And am I conscious of God seeking to break through to me? C.S. Lewis wrote, 'God whispers to us in our pleasures, speaks in our conscience, but shouts in our pains: it is His megaphone to rouse a deaf world.' In what is happening to us at the moment, is God whispering, speaking, or shouting? And more importantly, are we listening?

Most, like myself at one time, prefer not to listen to the Christian message, imagining it to be both irrational in our scientific age, and irrelevant to the modern world. In the next chapter, I want to try and challenge the first misconception, and in the following briefly examine the credibility of the sources for Christian Faith itself.

2

Reasons to Believe

A song I enjoyed when younger was Tim Hardin's 'Reasons to Believe,' sung of course by Rod Stewart. It begins,

'If I listened long enough to you
I'd find a way to believe that it's all true
Knowing that you lied straight-faced while I cried
Still I look to find a reason to believe.'

The words portray the persistence of a man who knows the woman he loves has lied, but still, he looks for reasons to believe her. The tension is between what is true, and what he wants to be true. Some have portrayed Christian faith this way: faith is believing when the evidence won't support it; or worse, believing what you know isn't true. Faith understood this way, can appear hopelessly naive or so emotional a response to life that while it works for some, other more rational persons need not take it too seriously.

In this chapter, I want to question the reasonableness of my faith by asking, 'is it not irrelevant in our modern scientific age, and incompatible with wider human experience?' To do this honestly, I want to ask four questions, which New Testament scholar Tom Wright suggests constitute one's 'world view.' In asking these questions I'm asking, 'Is my world-view credible?' The questions are: Who am I? Where am I? What is wrong? and, What is the solution? (Wright, 1992, 132-133).

Who am I?

This is of course the key existential question of life. A child answers it by giving their name; an adult knows that simple label represents more fully all that nature and nurture, life and learning, allow us to become. And yet, we grow conscious also of being able to resist and even surmount what can often feel like the given limitations of our lot. An honest exploration of the reasonableness of my faith must begin by asking if my backstory predisposed me to faith? If the sense of 'felt appointment' was indeed accurate, but humanly understandable?

It is certainly true that the culture into which I was born had strong religious aspects, but any positive predisposition to faith as a consequence seems highly unlikely. As I made clear to the young man I met, the religion I had witnessed left me completely disaffected.

This seems likely on another front too. The powerful impact of 'significant others' in our younger years is universally accepted. The key role of one's father, some have suggested, can inform the projection of a childish wish for the protection of a heavenly father. Relations with my father, in earlier years, were very strained. Although grateful for better relations now, my wish then to project such relations unto a divine father would have felt (to borrow Lewis's image) like a mouse hoping to find a cat. One wonders if these strained relations might have led to the imaginative invention of a more ideal heavenly substitute, or is the model just losing its explanatory power?

Another thought appeals as a better fit for the facts. In John 6v44, Jesus reacts to grumbling Jews who refuse him saying, *"No one can come to me unless the father who sent me draws him."* The word 'draw' (*helkyo*) can mean: physically, to 'drag,' as in John 21 where a large catch of fish is first 'hauled' into a boat (v6), then unto a beach (v11); or psychologically, to draw 'by inward power, or impel.'

My resistance to where I was being taken that night in Plymouth was obvious, but on another level, something was also driving me. Who of us has not wondered, 'there must be more to life than this?' During that period I was asking questions such as this, and if I'm honest, feeling a growing sense of dissatisfied longing for more than the usual distractions. Life had become a little like the cafe I had dropped into, but what I needed, I couldn't find on the menu. The great church father, St. Augustine, once prayed, "You have made us for yourself, and our hearts are restless until they find their rest in you."

Going back to the question we began with, "Who am I?" although the experience of that night was only a beginning, I came to the realisation I was somebody who needed God, and that need resonated within me as my young friend spoke and awakened, not a new interest but an old instinct that I already knew only God could satisfy. This brings us to the next question...

Where am I?

There was a time I would have thought the answer to such a question merely incidental. Our capacity to think and objectify can mistakenly convince us we are not essentially part of the environments we live in; just passing through. But as studies of the world's ecosystems show, we are all inextricably linked not only with other species but to the environment we inhabit. Indeed, the relationships of dependence that can be traced are utterly staggering, causing us to marvel not just at the complexity, but complementarity of it all.

If, as I've just suggested, something of God resonated within me, surely there should be evidence of his active presence around me? I have often thought this is the case. If we take first a question that has always intrigued me, namely, the origin of life, the provisionality of proposed scientific explanations are far from satisfying. For a start, it is only relatively recently, since the mid-twentieth century, that an explanation was thought necessary, as the eternity of the material world was the widely accepted notion. Now, due to the discoveries of an expanding universe, and the sound of background radiation thought evidence of a very early big-bang, opinion has completely swung the other way. Earth had a beginning!

So, we have a material world that began. But did that make the origin of organic, cellular life, inevitable? The dominant theory in the biological sciences presupposes the emergence of simpler life form(s), millions of years ago, that evolved to become more complex. But how easily can life's beginnings in the universe be explained? Are the material and non-material merely different points on the same continuum? John Lennox quotes geneticist Michael Denton: 'the break between the non-living and the living world 'represents the most dramatic and fundamental of all the discontinuities of nature. Between a living cell and the most highly ordered non-biological systems, such as a crystal or a snowflake, there is a chasm as vast and absolute as it is possible to conceive.' It was this point that led the late world-renowned British Philosopher, Anthony Flew, known for the rejection of non-naturalistic explanations for the origin of life, to abandon that position in his later years in favour of necessary causation from outside our biological systems. He says, that he simply, 'had to go where the evidence leads.'

The leap from non-life to life, or across that vast and absolute chasm, becomes even more mind-boggling when we try to conceive the complexity of just one living cell. Lennox quote's Denton again, 'Even the tiniest of bacterial cells, weighing less than a trillionth of a gram, is 'a veritable micro-miniaturised factory containing thousands of exquisitely designed pieces of intricate molecular machinery, made up altogether of 100 thousand million atoms, far more complicated than any machine built by man and absolutely without parallel in the non-living world'.

Although the massive question of the origin of life, finds (in my mind, at least) an only satisfactory answer when we look to God, the evidence for design too in the natural world also points to Him. McGrath, remarking on the precise range of constants that must coexist to make life in the universe possible, makes the point that if connected to some 'cosmic control panel,' and the settings nudged even slightly, 'we would not be here to discuss it.' He concludes, 'our universe seems to exist in an absurdly precise state compared to the available range of possible values' (McGrath, 2012, p.99). It's as though the universe knew we were coming!

Space prevents us from exploring so much more in the natural world that many have found pointers to God, such as the presence of order, regularity and rational intelligibility that makes the scientific enterprise possible and productive. Pointers to God, some argue, are present in aspects of human experience. We see that rationality eye-wateringly present in the discovery, for example, of DNA. This information processing molecule in the cells of living things stores the instructions needed for the creation of a particular organism. The chemical code (or genome) for a human being has only four letters but is over three billion letters long. Says Prof. John Lennox, 'If a printed, meaningful menu cannot be generated by mindless natural processes but needs the input of a mind, what are we to say about the human genome? Does it not much more powerfully point to an origin in a mind - the mind of God?'

Christian revelation announces 'In the beginning, God created the heavens and the earth,' (Genesis 1v1). We're told that a series of creative feats brought into being life in all its ascending complexity, and ultimately life capable of reproducing itself. Mankind was created, (2v7), out of materials discernibly present in the natural world. However, there was 'breathed into his nostrils the breath of life, and man became a living being.' I find here a precise beginning to life; an explanation of both its variation and replication. I find, in a phraseology I cannot fully understand, an explanation for the emergence of living cells that nothing else present at their appearance can explain.

Scientific findings are not something that necessarily calls into question the existence of God, but rather shows *how* he achieves what he does. When science proposes the likelihood of certain explanations for the natural world, unless they have a very suspect BBE date, the response need not be, "Oh, there isn't a God after all!"But rather, "Ah, so this is how He does it!" Because this is so, as to the question, "Where am I?" the answer must be: in a world suffused from its beginnings, with the presence and power of God.

What is wrong?

During the years after the Second World War, the London Times invited readers to propose answers to the following question: 'What is wrong with the world?' A well-known respondent replied: 'Dear Sir, in response to your question, 'What is wrong with the world? I am!' Yours Sincerely, G.K. Chesterton.' In this small exchange, The Times believes something is wrong with the world, and Chesterton that something is wrong with him that partially at least explains the world's problems.

That something is wrong with both the world and ourselves, is self-evident. As I write we are living through a major pandemic that has taken countless lives worldwide. The numbers of those contracting cancers seem to be growing. Not so many years ago we were all reeling at the news of a Tsunami that took the lives of hundreds of thousands. In this catalogue of human loss, lives taken by war in the 20th

Century alone, exceed those taken in all previous centuries on record. With the serious depletion of natural resources, the threat of extinction for some species, and the large scale pollution of the planet, who could believe that there isn't something wrong? Stephen Hawking's suggestion, even if tongue in cheek, that the only hope for the human race is to populate another planet, seems shockingly reasonable. So, what is wrong?

In our previous discussion, we thought a little about the rational intelligibility and order of the natural world and living things. So ordered is it, its structure and processes are capable of being represented in mathematical forms that are intelligible to us, and by which the world can communicate its deepest secrets. The Christian Faith sees the reason for these rationalities both in the world and in ourselves, as pointing to the creative intelligence behind both. But it goes further. Christian Faith affirms, the reason there is something wrong both with ourselves and in the world, is that humanity has rebelled against this personal, creative intelligence. Paul, the apostle, speaks of our being 'separated' and 'alienated from God,' (Ephesians 4v18; Colossians 1v21). Taking into account the wider biblical perspective, 'this rebellion reflects a cosmic dislocation between the creator and the creation, and the world is consequently out of tune with its created intention,' (Wright, 1992, 133).

When children are very young their necessary self-centredness can mean they mistakenly see themselves responsible for the most arbitrary events. But Chesterton is not indulging the same childish naivety when he says that he, and we, are wrong with the world; he's recognising profound solidarity between ourselves and our environment that has brought it down with us.

Paul the apostle wrote, *'Therefore, just as sin came into the world through one man, and death through sin, and so death spread to all men because all sinned...'* (Romans 5v12). His point is that sin entered the world and brought death with it. That death, far from merely human and physical, describes the broken relations between ourselves and the creator, and a 'bondage to decay' the earth both suffers with, and longs to be 'liberated from' (8v21). Although some find such an explanation unacceptable, the universal entropy that we all witness daily within and without presses its relevance upon us.

What is the solution?

As this whole chapter is an attempt to provide rational credibility to my faith, I cannot help but feel hope rise within me. When I first embraced Christ, it admittedly involved strong subjective elements. Alister McGrath, in his book, *'Mere Apologetics'*, shares his faith journey. Unlike myself, he denies becoming a Christian because of any felt need for God. He says he was someone who 'believed there was only stagnant pond-water to drink, who then discovered champagne, (2012, 176).

So what is this champagne? What is the Christian solution? If what is wrong originates with ourselves and alienates us from our creator, the solution must in essence be a reconciliation. If what is wrong also impacts our environment, the solution must extend out into that environment. When we turn to the NT, we discover just such a solution; it begins, not with ourselves, but with the creator who acts for us. He initiates such a programme of recovery that not only are we transformed from within, but a new social order is born with a new and restored environment to inhabit.

Before we look more closely at the first element of this recovery, a personal transformation from within, we need to explore the reasonableness of my newfound faith further by examining briefly, the sources for it: its literature and its leading figure, Jesus Christ.

3

The One who got it Right

The Christian bible has occupied a significant place in British society. The old King James Version has bequeathed us words and expressions we simply take for granted not always knowing their origin. Every time we 'put words into someone's mouth' or 'see the writing on the wall' or 'cast the first stone' or call someone 'the salt of the earth,' - we quote this older version.

If we have to give testimony in a court of law, we will be offered a bible to swear on. And we'd be in good company as Elizabeth 11 also swore on one when crowned Queen in 1953. Indeed, she was handed a bible by the Archbishop, with the words, "we present you with this Book, the most valuable thing that this world affords." If we lesser mortals visit a hotel, remarkably for our day, there is some likelihood we'll find a Gideon bible in a bedside drawer. And yet, although the bible has been a best seller for literally centuries; one cannot help but feel its place in society is more a concession to the past, than a reflection of present sympathies.

So, what is the bible? It is a collection of books, 66 in all, 39 of which Christian's call the Old Testament (OT), and the remaining 27 they call the New Testament (NT). The literary make-up of the OT is varied, but the fundamental backdrop to it all is the religious *history* of Israel.

This history begins with God's call of Abraham to leave a city called Ur and journey to Canaan. While there, 'the Lord appeared to Abraham and said, "To your offspring, I will give this land." His offspring do finally settle as a people in that region, with Jerusalem ultimately becoming the nation's capital. The kingdom first functions as a monarchy then split into two kingdoms. In time, the Northern Kingdom is invaded by Assyria and its inhabitants were deported, and never seen again. Later, the Southern Kingdom is invaded and its citizens were deported to Babylon.

In time, and with the rise of the Persian King, Cyrus, the Jewish exiles were allowed to return to their land, rebuild their temple, and establish themselves once again as a nation. Many years later they are invaded by Rome and become that Empire's eastern frontier, as Britain also did, to the west.

The OT is, therefore, rooted in history. Indeed, the British Museum houses artefacts and inscriptions that illustrate some of it. The capture of Jerusalem, for example, is recorded on the 'Babylonian Chronicle' (a clay tablet) telling us Nebuchadnezzar 'encamped against the city of Judah and on the second day of the month Adar, he seized the city and captured the king (Jehoiachin). He appointed there a king of his own choice (Zedekiah), received its heavy tribute and sent (them) to Babylon.' So, the Chronicle dates events recorded in 2 Kings 24v8-17, to 16th March 597 BC. The Museum also houses the 'Cyrus Cylinder' which records the policy of Cyrus allowing exiles in Babylon to return home, confirming what we read of the event for Jews, in Ezra 6v3-5.

The OT is of course not just history. It records God's *revelation* of himself to Israel, through their history. Abraham we've mentioned, but Moses also received revelations from God, personally and as the people's leader. The revelation on Mt Sinai, and reception of the Law, was to show the people how the God of their fathers expected a grateful people to live who had just been delivered from slavery in Egypt. The problem was that Israel, throughout its history, fell far short of grateful. As a consequence, it frequently suffered judgement for its ungodly ways. These judgements, whether natural or political, generally provoked a cry to the Lord for deliverance. And again he would graciously respond to forgive and restore.

If we look closely, the same pattern emerges in Israel's walk before God: Rebellion - Retribution - Restitution - Restoration - and Rebellion, again! The cycle exposes a fundamental moral weakness, best described by Jeremiah when he wrote, *'The heart is deceitful above all things, and desperately sick; who can understand it?'* (Jeremiah 17v9). So, what's to be done?

This brings us to one last literary genre in the OT, and that is **prophecy**. It is clear that an 'arrangement' that addressed both the people's sin and their need for power to faithfully serve, was necessary. What is to happen? In Isaiah 53 we have the most extraordinary account of One who is to come, a Servant, who would make restitution, and achieve lasting restoration for Israel. It is with the announcement that this expected figure has come that the NT opens. Picking up on one word in the original, dear to Isaiah (61v1), Mark begins his biography of Jesus, 'The beginning of the 'good news' about Jesus the Messiah, the Son of God, as it is written in Isaiah the prophet...'

In what remains of this chapter, we will explore the figure of Christ under the headings: His life, death, resurrection, and return; commenting on the reliability of the biblical narrative concerning each.

His Life

Given that Christ conducted his three-year public ministry confined to a country roughly the size of Wales, it is frankly staggering to think of the influence he has brought to bear on human history. Space prevents us from considering much, but art, music, literature, education, science and social welfare throughout the western world, directly or indirectly, owe their original inspiration in some form to Christ and his teaching.

And neither is this inspiration merely a matter of history; it impacts profoundly the way we live today; even if not always consciously felt. Tom Holland, the historian, (who does not claim Christian Faith) in his recent book *'Dominion - The Making of the Modern Mind'* writes of what he calls 'the most enduring and influential legacy of the ancient world, a revolution in values that has proven transformative like nothing else in history: Christianity.'

When we consider the sources for what is believed about this life, its 'expectedness' strikes us from the outset. When his parents take him to the temple for dedication, an elderly figure 'waiting for the consolation of Israel,' declares, *'Sovereign Lord, ...my eyes have seen your salvation, which you have prepared in the sight of all nations: a light for revelation to the Gentiles and the glory of your people Israel'* (Luke 2v25, 30-32).

At the age of approximately 30, Jesus begins a ministry that in word and deed proclaim his identity and calling as Israel's end-time deliverer. What is remarkable is how Christ saves. Yes, as we will see, he died to save, but first, he lived to save. It was proper for him, he says as he submits to baptism, *'...to fulfil all righteousness'* (Matthew 3v15). Israel repeatedly failed to fulfil the righteous calling of God upon it, but here is one who assumes that same calling, and succeeds.

In the gospels, and later NT, Christ identifies with those he saves by first living the lives they should but failed to. It's this that makes his innocence in both life and death, so essential to his call. Indeed, moves him to say something that on any other lips would invite derision, *'The one who sent me is with me; he has not left me alone, for I always do what pleases him,'* (John 8v29). Whereas Israel's history was often marked by a sense of divine withdrawal, due to its sin, Christ's life is marked by the Father's presence, for he 'always did what pleases him.'

Now can we honestly believe that such a life has been lived? Nothing we see in ourselves, or the world around us, encourages us to think so. But the NT insists that what it records is history; this life was lived. Two of the four gospel writers, Matthew and John, were recognised as eyewitnesses to the matter they record, by the early church. Mark, we're told by Papias, a friend of the apostle John, wrote as he was informed by Peter; and the gospel's internal evidence supports that claim. Luke complied a narrative *'of the things that have been accomplished among us, just as those who from the beginning were eyewitnesses and ministers of the word have delivered them to us,'* (1v1-4).

Christ and his followers are also referred to by some non-biblical sources, within the late first - early second century AD. Among them are the Jewish historian, Josephus, and the Roman historians, Tacitus and Suetonius, and diarist, Pliny the Younger. While these testimonies don't oblige us to believe all that the gospel writers wrote, they do oblige us to accept a historical core to their accounts. When we struggle to believe some of what is said, such as miracles, because as we say, 'these things simply don't happen,' we have to remember that the gospel writers would agree, and add, 'That's our point; in this case, and with this person, they did! And so, we've written about it.

His Death

Among the more remarkable details, again easily missed, is the space the gospel writers devote to Christ's death. If I bought a biography of a favourite historical figure and discovered over 35% of the book was about their death and funeral, I'd be unhappy. It's their life achievements I want to hear about! And that of course, is what the gospel writers want us to see: his death was his crowning achievement. In Mark, Jesus puts it this way, *'the Son of Man came not to be served but to serve, and to give his life as a ransom for many'* (10v45). It's this gospel emphasis upon Christ fulfilling in himself the roles of both the righteous and suffering servant, that we see how thoroughly he acted for his people, fulfilling their vocation, and yet taking divine judgment in their place.

Before moving on, it's vital to notice that the NT doesn't present Christ principally as a moral inspiration, a social reformer, or indeed any other figure designed to improve our life performance. Rather, he came to live the life we fail to, and die the death we deserve to. The mission of Christ in life and death was not simply to inspire our moral improvement, but to effect our deliverance and moral transformation (Romans 8v1-4).

When we read of the crucifixion in the gospels, certain details give it the ring of truth. From the start, the Jews have to defer to Roman authority if the death sentence is to be passed. The way crucifixion as a process takes place: the victim carrying his crossbeam, nails piercing his hands and feet, the sign proclaiming his charge, and the soldier not needing to break his legs to accelerate death; the bodily release of blood and water, or clot and serum that separate upon death, and signify it has taken place; and the removal of the victim before the sabbath begins. These reasons, historically, religiously and anatomically appropriate, have the ring of authentic reporting, and inspire textual confidence.

His Resurrection

With the resurrection, we encounter difficulties many find insurmountable, and so we must begin acknowledging that the disciples found it equally baffling. Not only did Thomas refuse to believe until the evidence was compelling, but the entire apostolic band would have struggled given the absence of any expectation that such a resurrection as Christ's would happen. Indeed, when the women first came and reported what they found (or didn't find) at the tomb, we read that they did not believe the women, because their words seemed to them like nonsense, (Luke 24v11). This makes sense, as Jewish expectations of resurrection were of *all* the righteous, on the *last* day. In the gospel record, where we find the promise of Jesus that he would die and rise again, the reaction of hearers is to his death; as this was not how the Messiah's role was popularly understood. The 'rising' would almost certainly be interpreted as Mary did at Lazarus's death, *'I know he will rise again at the resurrection at the last day,'* (John 11v24).

Added to this, we again find in the gospel accounts something easily overlooked, but having the ring of truth. The writers simply record what happened, and leave later theological reflection to others. Even in Matthew, his usual 'this is that' approach, tying events to prophesy, is conspicuously absent when it comes to recording the resurrection. However, we do read of the very human responses of fear, bewilderment, astonishment and joy, (Matthew 28v8,10; Mark 16v8; Luke 24v37,41; John 20v20); and even the very honest admission, that 'some doubted,' (Matthew 28v17).

Certain apparent textual difficulties are sometimes raised. It's true that across the gospels different numbers of female witnesses are mentioned. As there are no contradictions, but just an enlargement of the same group, this arguably strengthens the testimony. Indeed, using female witnesses at all suggests truthfulness, rather than fabrication, as their testimony in a court of law was discounted. It has been pointed out that John tells us, 'while it was still dark, Mary Magdalene went to the tomb' (John 20v1), while Mark says, 'just after sunrise, they were on their way..,' (Mark 15v2), but as more than one commentator suggests, this merely reflects the possibility of two different times on the same journey.

A fascinating account of Peter and another disciple reaching the tomb is given in John. We read, 'Both of them were running together, but the other disciple outran Peter and reached the tomb first. And stooping to look in, he saw the linen cloths lying there, but he did not go in. Then Simon Peter came, following him, and went into the tomb. He saw the linen cloths lying there, and the face cloth, which had been on Jesus' head, not lying with the linen cloths but folded up in a place by itself,' (John 20v4-7). The incidental detail as to who outran who is interesting, but hardly vital, unless it was remembered. As for the cloths, we find them placed apart, in just the way they would have been when applied to the body of Jesus.

It's often said that there were no actual witnesses to the resurrection, and that of course is true. What was witnessed was the resurrected Jesus. But look at the variety in the testimony: there were individuals, pairs, groups, and indeed, 'five hundred brothers at one time' (1 Corinthians 15v6). It's remarkable too that Paul adds, 'most of whom are still alive, though some have fallen asleep' - this of course implies the possibility of verification! It's true, of course, that we are straying out of the gospels in sourcing Paul, but this particular testimony is the closest chronological account we have to the resurrection. Paul writes about twenty years after the event and describes it as 'what I have received I passed unto you,' confirming that in such a short time-frame the resurrection of Jesus had become a defining belief for his earliest followers. As James Dunn (Uni. of Durham) writes, 'this tradition, we can be entirely confident, was formulated as tradition, within months of Jesus' death (2003, p.855).

It is of course possible that the earliest witnesses genuinely believed that Jesus had risen, but were deceived rather than deceiving. Some have thought it more likely that the earliest experiences were of grief-induced visions or hallucinations, the mind creating what it wants to see, rather than sees. The number of witnesses, together with the variety of settings argues against this.

It could also be that the written records are unintentionally inaccurate. Scholarship reminds us that the earliest testimonies to Christ's life were in fact, oral testimonies; and that in itself casts doubt on the accuracy of what was passed on, as any game of Chinese whispers will show. Such a low view of oral transmission might even suggest the Jesus of the gospels is more legend than history. So, what can be said?

We need to recall that this period of oral transmission wasn't entirely without the regulative control of the written text. Paul's earlier mention shows that within two decades resurrection was committed to writing, meaning 'there was little to no time for the early Christian view of Jesus to change, before being inscribed by Paul,' (Boyd & Eddy, 2007, 67). Papias, an early church father believed to have known the apostle John, reports Matthew acting as 'a designated note-taker among the earliest disciples' (Eusebius in: Boyd & Eddy, 69).

The fact remains that the earliest testimonies were inevitably by word of mouth. However, rather than a weak point in any argument for later textual reliability, the opposite can be true. Studies into transmission in orally dominant cultures point out the high degree of accuracy involved in the process, given that stories often embodied truth fundamental to a groups identity. In conclusion, the short period of oral transmission before a textual record of Christ's resurrection presents far less a reason to doubt the reliability of the witnesses than was first thought. Added to this, any question that the later texts were a corruption of earlier ones simply doesn't hold up under the overwhelming agreement of the many texts we have. None of the minor variations in content that exist alter the meaning of what's recorded. It has to be said, this is unparalleled among ancient texts available to us today.

Now, does all we've considered demand we believe the resurrection happened? No! However, it demonstrates two incontestable facts: the belief was thought evidentially based among earliest Christians; and secondly, is commended to believers today, not because they will find it helpful, or comforting, but because it happened, and will happen for all who trust the resurrected and living Jesus today.

His Return

We come now, not to what *has* happened, but what we're told *will* happen. Christian belief in the return of Christ can seem as fantastic as his resurrection. But as I write, we are experiencing a pandemic as universal in its reach, as the promised event of the return of Christ. And rather than only a promise by him, it is integrally linked to who he saw himself to be; his very identity. Jesus referred to himself, most often, as the Son of Man. It's a title that, although a possible reference only to his humanity, clearly meant more.

The figure first appears in the book of Daniel. In Daniel 7 we read of a figure who *'was one like a son of man, coming with the clouds of heaven'* (v13). This enigmatic figure, we're told, was given 'authority, glory and sovereign power; all people, nations and men of every language worshipped him.... and his kingdom will be one that will never be destroyed,' (v14). In Matthew 24v30 Jesus identifies himself as this end-time figure, 'the Son of Man' who all will see, 'coming on the clouds of heaven with power and great glory.' There's little doubt the earliest Christian's were encouraged by Jesus to believe he would come again.

When I reflect on the ministry I've heard, I have to admit the Return of Christ has not featured prominently. And yet, with the ravages of the present pandemic some who have never given once-fantastical ideas like 'the end of the world' a thought, are now asking, not 'if' but 'when.' When the bible discusses the return of Christ, it does so with a view to both the judgement of the human race and for those who have embraced him as Lord, settlement in a new heavens and new earth. In this new setting both natural and moral decay, indeed entropy of any kind will have been banished; and all things made new.

Conclusion

The purpose of this chapter, and the previous one, was to show that first of all, in the natural world, and then secondly, in the Christian Scripture, and the figure of Christ, there are genuine 'reasons to believe.' Reasons, that although different to the very subjective experience on my night of encounter in Plymouth, nevertheless provide some rational support for 'the leap of faith.' For myself, the leap of faith wasn't 'a leap in the dark.' There are good rational reasons for believing, that not merely encourage faith, but enlarge and extend the journey experience sets us out on.

In the next chapter, we will explore a section of the gospel narrative that takes us to the heart of what Christ does in the life he transforms.

4

The Heart of the Matter

As I said before, the times have changed since those early days in a country village. When I discuss the past with my father, now in his mid-eighties, and ask him to compare the times, the answer is nearly always, "Earlier days were often hard, and few pretended; today, all is pretence." This can be a hard case to answer. Media and advertising, to be effective, inevitably make more of everything than is warranted; and we all breathe its air, and speak its language.

The sad consequence of all of this is that the confidence levels of many are falling in what is happening around them. We're asking more and more often, is this just another bigging up exercise, or is something of substance at stake? Such questions are also asked of the church, which all too often succumbs to the same rhetoric and mindset of the world. It too sounds just as committed to the hype and the same excessive use of superlatives as the societies it ministers to. So here is the question: is there anything real at the heart of the Christian message? Is it possible to experience God, or is that just another manipulation of language?

To explore further this theme, I can think of no better passage to help us than John's gospel, 3v1-15. Here, the same theme is referred to by the words, *born again* or *born from above*. Let's listen to these words of Jesus the teacher and see if they have any application to our life journey.

In the ESV the passage reads as follows:

Now there was a man of the Pharisees named Nicodemus, a ruler of the Jews. This man came to Jesus by night and said to him,

"Rabbi, we know that you are a teacher come from God, for no one can do these signs that you do unless God is with him."

Jesus answered him, "Truly, truly, I say to you, unless one is born again he cannot see the kingdom of God." Nicodemus said to him, "How can a man be born when he is old? Can he enter a second time into his mother's womb and be born?"

Jesus answered, "Truly, truly, I say to you, unless one is born of water and the Spirit, he cannot enter the kingdom of God. That which is born of the flesh is flesh, and that which is born of the Spirit is spirit. Do not marvel that I said to you, 'You must be born again.' The wind blows where it wishes, and you hear its sound, but you do not know where it comes from or where it goes. So it is with everyone who is born of the Spirit."

Nicodemus said to him, "How can these things be?"

Jesus answered him, "Are you the teacher of Israel and yet you do not understand these things? Truly, truly, I say to you, we speak of what we know, and bear witness to what we have seen, but you do not receive our testimony. If I have told you earthly things and you do not believe, how can you believe if I tell you heavenly things? No one has ascended into heaven except he who descended from heaven, the Son of Man. And as Moses lifted up the serpent in the wilderness, so must the Son of Man be lifted up, that whoever believes in him may have eternal life.

So, how does this exchange between Nicodemus and Jesus shed light on all true encounters with God, both ancient and modern?

We should probably notice, first, that it's the author's declared intention that what he has written, will lead to knowing God. John tells readers, in 20v31, that he writes *'so that you may believe that Jesus is the Christ, the Son of God and that by believing you may have life in his name.'* Getting this point raises a legitimate expectation of this passage - discovering what he calls, 'life.' This word is a favourite of John's; it's the Greek word *'zoe'* which refers not merely to our physical or even interior lives, but life as it was meant to be; life in relationship with God.

And so, at the outset of these things, one question deserves an honest answer: 'am I open to the possibility that life as it was meant to be, can be found in a relationship with God?' If not, we have to accept that it may not be Christ who falls short, but the limits we place on what's possible.

We should also notice, secondly, who it is who comes to Jesus in this passage. We're told his name, Nicodemus, and that he is *'a Pharisee.'* Pharisees were, at their best, diligent observers of the Jewish Law. Nicodemus has even more to commend him; he is also *'a ruler of the Jews.'* This we can assume meant he was greatly respected among the people. Here is a man of authority and learning; what he said, people listened to.

All this makes what we're told next, intriguing - *'he came to Jesus by night.'* We're bound to ask, 'why by night?' He was certainly inquisitive about the impact Jesus was having on the people at large. In the previous chapter *'many believed in his name when they saw the signs that he was doing.'* Nicodemus feels God must be in this. However, the majority of Pharisees were far from persuaded; to the very end, many opposed Jesus.

One reasonable conclusion, therefore, might be that Nicodemus was trying to avoid the attention of his fellow Pharisees. Later, we learn of another who was 'a secret disciple.' Like that Pharisee, maybe Nicodemus thought exposure too costly. I recall, in my early days at college, hiding a NT in a magazine that others in the student union bar might not notice; and make unwelcome assumptions. To my horror, a young female Malaysian student came up behind me, noticed the NT, and announced in the hearing of all present, "You are a Christian! How wonderful!" I certainly didn't feel wonderful. For Nicodemus too, that kind of exposure may have been too early.

But surely this is an attitude we can all identify with. It is a 'given' that we all want the approval of our peers. From the school playground to the upper echelons of academia - no one likes rejection. This conviction certainly explains why I also refused to discuss my night-time encounter with anyone onboard the ship. And yet, Nicodemus at least risked the suspicion, if not yet the censure of his group. This surely challenges us all to ask: how independent are we of the pressures around us, in the search for what's true?

This brings us to notice the exchange between Nicodemus and Jesus. *'Rabbi, we know that you are a teacher come from God, for no one can do these signs that you do unless God is with him.'* Notice the respect Nicodemus shows Jesus, he calls him Rabbi. The title means 'teacher.' It amounts to something on the lips of one who others might address as the Very Revd Dr.

Nicodemus's respect surely speaks to us. If we are to come to Jesus to be taught, no matter what our credentials, the first requirement is surely to pay him the respect of listening to what he says. I'm often surprised, not that so many reject Jesus - he said they would - but that so many do so with seemingly little understanding of who they're rejecting, as the briefest conversations usually show.

But notice too, the unexpected response of Jesus. Most would be grateful for the respect a man like Nicodemus shows, but Jesus launches into correcting him: *'unless one is born again he cannot see the kingdom of God.'* Jesus is telling Nicodemus that whatever he thinks he understands about the workings of God, he doesn't. In fact, not only is the true activity of God incomprehensible to him but inaccessible, for without the new birth, *'no one can even enter the Kingdom.'*

I wonder how Nicodemus felt at this correction by Jesus. Often correction by another makes us defensive. Instead of quietly submitting to the thought 'I might not understand. I must listen carefully,' we can question our opponent's credibility with thoughts like, 'who does he think he is, anyway?' or conclude, 'what nonsense!' I wonder if Nicodemus chooses the second approach when he asks next, *'How can a man be born when he is old? Can he enter a second time into his mother's womb and be born?'*

What Nicodemus is coming to see is that although being born again is a necessity, it is also a human impossibility. Its necessity can be seen first in Nicodemus himself. If anyone had an intellectual and cultural advantage here, it's Him. He was a recognised expert in things religious, and yet he couldn't see or enter the kingdom. Not only that, but he and his fellow Pharisees so esteemed God's law that if obeying rules was how to experience God, they'd cracked it - but Jesus is saying - they haven't.

We should slow down here, for the implications of what Jesus is saying are revolutionary and utterly counter-intuitive to what we all generally think an experience of God is about. First, it's not something we achieve; either because we are religiously active in a way others aren't, or excel morally where others haven't. We may even enjoy the cultural advantage of being brought up in a Christian environment, by Christian parents. We might spend our whole lives in such circles

(Nicodemus certainly did), even take part in church activities, and be baptised. But none of these things, or their collective worth, amounts to being born again. Isn't this shocking! And to come to see it is hard, as Nicodemus illustrates because our natural religiosity rejects it.

Paul, an apostle of Jesus, came to see this and rejected such imagined advantages in himself, to acquire what was of true worth: *'If someone else thinks they have reasons to put confidence in the flesh, I have more,'* and he calls himself, *'a Hebrew of Hebrews; regarding the law, a Pharisee; as for zeal, persecuting the church; as for righteousness based on the law, faultless. But whatever were gains to me - I now consider loss.'* (Philippians 3v4-7 NIV). Paul is saying all this imagined personal, cultural and moral capital just got in the way of knowing God; and for that reason, he called it *'excrement'* (v8), which had to be rejected.

So, the first thing Jesus teaches is that the new birth is a necessity; and with the help of Nicodemus, that it is also a human impossibility, for *'How can a man be born when he is old?'* The answer is, humanly speaking, he can't! A man once asked the 18th Century revivalist preacher, George Whitfield, why he preached so often on *'You must be born again.'* Can you guess his answer? "Because," he said, "You must be born again."

Now we're in a position to notice the Lord's explanation. *'Jesus answers, "Truly, truly, I say to you, unless one is born of water and the Spirit, he cannot enter the kingdom of God. That which is born of the flesh is flesh, and that which is born of the Spirit is spirit..."'*

At the heart of this explanation is a contrast over methods of reproduction. Our physical selves can give birth to new physical life - flesh gives birth to flesh! But this is also true, says Jesus, in another dimension: *'spirit gives birth to Spirit!'*

It's the Holy Spirit who performs this reproductive act. We find this anticipated in the biblical footnote to the *new birth;* it reads, 'or *from above.*' Jesus is saying, an encounter with God is an experience he initiates. Now, this point is critical. Whatever being 'born again' means, it produces children, born *'not of natural descent, nor human decision or a husband's will, but born of God,'* (John 1v11-12). So what kind of experience is 'spirit giving birth to spirit'?

First, by using the words 'water and spirit' it's fair to conclude that Jesus, at the very least, means a deeply *inward* event. Support for this is found in John 7 where *'streams of living water that flow from within,'* are a reference to *'the Spirit which those who believed in him were later to receive'* (7v39). The point is this, on any reading, the new birth is a deeply *inward* event.

Secondly, this inwardness also makes clear another characteristic of new birth, 'it is an image of absolute transformation' (Keener, 2003, p.552). It reflects not just a fresh start on an old journey, but quite literally - a beginning again. This thought speaks loudly to the battered remains of so many sincere resolutions to change ourselves. Deep and lasting behavioural change, laughs at the thought that a mere decision can overturn what a lifetime of decision-making has made us. Only the Holy Spirit, applying to us, what Jesus has done for us, brings about a 'new creation.' It's this transformation that we are to understand by the image of new-birth.

Thirdly, this inward transformation, if it is to bring us into a living relationship with God, must have within it the power to release us from the destructive thinking and behaviours of our past, and empower a better future. This is exactly what we find new birth does when we explore the origins of *'water and spirit'* as a pairing in the bible Jesus used, our Old Testament. The images appear together in Ezekiel 36v25-27, and the subject is the new work of grace God will perform in the days of the Messiah's reign.

Ezekiel writes, *'I will gather you (and) I will sprinkle clean water on you and…cleanse you from all your impurities… I will give you a new heart and put a new spirit in you.. and move you to follow my decrees'* (Ezekiel 36 v25-27).

The water is a symbolic reference to cleansing from all impurities or the removal of sin. Jesus probably expected Nicodemus, an expert in Temple practices, like the use of ceremonial waters, to understand the connection between clean water, cleansing from sin, and forgiveness. What forgiveness means we will explore in the next chapter, but we can at least recognise what it achieves, our release from what prevents a new beginning with God.

What about the Spirit? When the spirit is given, Ezekiel says, he will (v27) *'move people to follow God's decrees.'* In other words, he will motivate those he acts upon, to want to follow God's path. It's like the giving of a *new heart*, that gives rise to new desires, new aspirations that one did not previously have. And this new desire is from God, and for God.

The apostle Paul teaches the same in his letter to Titus: whatever knowing God entails, it is *'not because of works done by us (but) by the washing of regeneration and renewal of the Holy Spirit…'* Here, Water and Spirit are mentioned by way of their effects, 'washing and renewal', or 'forgiveness and spiritual anointing.' Here then is the two-fold experience Jesus reduces to the verbal phrase *born again* or *born from above.*

We also find this experience focused exclusively on the preaching of the infant church in Acts. The good news it proclaimed was that forgiveness and the gift of the Spirit was now available. Peter, in the first-ever Christian sermon, (Acts

2v38), calls hearers to faith *'in the name of Jesus Christ, for the forgiveness of your sins. And you will receive the gift of the Holy Spirit.'* And because these gifts are to be available throughout history (v39), *'the promise is for you and your children, and for all who are far off - for all whom the Lord our God will call.'*

I think we need to slow down and ponder the implications of what is being said by Jesus. For a start, whatever encountering God is, again it is not essentially something we do. The wind of the Spirit does blow with no one knowing where it comes from or where it goes. As a Pastor, I find this working of the Spirit almost always discernible in those who come to talk about faith. It's as though even the realisation of our need, that moves us to consciously repent and ask for forgiveness, is somehow mysteriously present in the Spirit drawing near. Seldom do any come merely wanting to discuss the content of the faith, but rather, convicted or exercised about God, and their position before him.

Having noticed the stress of Jesus on the essentially Spiritual work of new birth, we now need to reflect on the one direction Jesus does give Nicodemus. God may be the one who saves, however the gospel leaves us in no doubt as to how we enjoy the benefit of it. In John 3v14 Jesus says, *'Just as Moses lifted up the snake in the wilderness, so the Son of Man must be lifted up, that everyone who believes may have eternal life in him.'* To explore this, we turn now in the next chapter, to 'the good news.'

5
The Good News

By now we may have felt the challenge posed by Nicodemus's apparent advantages, and yet his exclusion from the life of God. We might feel, "it's all a bit much; why bother?" But notice Nicodemus isn't left demoralised, and neither are we.

Recently my wife and I were invited by friends to join them on a holiday in Jordan. For most who visit that country, the ancient city of Petra is the highlight, with its famous treasury facade that we associate with Indiana Jones and *Raiders of the Lost Ark*. Another popular site is the Wadi Rum, a moon-like desert-scape punctuated with vast cathedrals of stone that just emerge from below the earth's surface. Many associate this region with another Hollywood production, *The Martian*, starring Matt Damon. These modern associations pale into insignificance however when we realise that this landscape was the backdrop to ancient Israel's historic wilderness wanderings, out of Egypt to the promised land.

That journey, which ought to have taken weeks, instead took years, because of their grumbling at God and disbelief. In one of these incidents, recorded in Numbers 21, the people grumble so much the Lord sends venomous snakes among them. In response to the severity of this judgment, the people come repenting to Moses who petitions God on their behalf. The Lord relents, and instructs Moses (v8-9), *'Make a snake and put it up on a pole; anyone who is bitten can look at it and live.'* In response to the Lord's promise, *'Moses made a bronze*

*snake and put it up on a pole. Then when anyone was bitten
and looked at the bronze snake, they lived.'*

Today, on Mt. Nebo in Jordan, the site where Moses saw
but was prevented from entering the promised land, a model
of just such a snake stands. Beneath it are these very words of
Jesus from John 3. While there's little evidence that Jesus and
Nicodemus ever spoke on Mt Nebo, we can still appreciate
the message those who erected the model were conveying
- the true promised land, what John calls eternal life, still
awaits those who look to Christ, and live.

In essence, the words of Jesus tell us how life with God
is secured. It involves, first, something that *must* happen to
him, and as a consequence, something that *may* happen to
us. Let's look at each in order.

What happened to Jesus?

Jesus himself tells us, *'the Son of Man must be lifted.'* There
can be no doubt that he is talking about his crucifixion. In
John 12v32 he says as much – *'And I, when I am lifted up
from the earth, will draw all people to myself...'* (and John
adds) *'He said this to show the kind of death he was going to
die.'* Crucifixion was one of the cruellest, most barbaric forms
of execution known to the ancient world. So much so that
respectable Roman citizens, despite belonging to a culture
that perfected it, preferred not to talk of it, or subject their
own to it. It was preserved for the worst offenders; those
thought a threat to the Roman State. As it happens, the NT
accounts of the crucifixion of Jesus are the most extensive
and detailed we have of it from ancient times.

In the gospel accounts, it's clear that Jesus is arrested,
sentenced and executed for claiming a kingship that ostensibly
threatened peace in Israel and Roman authority with it. Not
all went along with the charge; notably, the Roman Governor,

Pilate, who although lacking the courage of his convictions, very graphically washed his hands of the affair, (Matthew 27v24). Nevertheless, Jesus was handed over to his accusers and suffered death on a cross.

What strikes us most in the biblical narrative is that although, as Pilate knew, Jesus was innocent of the charges made against him, and although *'wicked men took him and nailed him to the cross,'* nevertheless, says Peter, *'he was handed over... by God's set purpose and foreknowledge'* (Acts 2v23). In other words, not only were his executioners doing something but so too was God. If we ask what, it is again no better put than by Peter: *'For Christ also suffered once for sins, the righteous for the unrighteous, to bring you to God.'* Peter is saying, Jesus the righteous, acted for the unrighteous; he took their place. On the cross, their sins and the judgement they attract was taken by him. Jesus was *'lifted up'* to be a sacrifice for the sins of us all.

Here, in essence, is the reconciliation that constitutes the gospel's solution to mankind's problem. The hostility of God towards hostile sinners, he has himself visited on his Son (Romans 5v9) and having done so, he has opened up a way for us to bury our hostility and *'be reconciled to God'* (2 Corinthians 5v20).

What can happen to us?

Now, what does this mean in practical terms? It means that nothing need now prevent you or me from approaching God the Father, in the name of Jesus the Son. We can all have a relationship with God, by this new and living way that has been opened up for us, through his death. The NT sees sins as debts we owe God; and as it happens, so do our consciences. But these debts, or *'the charge of our legal indebtedness'* (Colossians 2v14), has been *'nailed to the cross'* where Jesus paid it in full. This cross-action in the mind of Jesus and his apostles is the ground upon which God can forgive us all our sins. To those, Jesus is saying, who can look to him, lifted up, 'there is therefore now no condemnation,' but rather 'peace with God, through our Lord Jesus Christ.'

If we ask, how does that relationship begin? Jesus says, just as the bronze snake was lifted on a pole, that all who looked might live, so the Son Man has been lifted up on his cross that 'all who believe may have eternal life in him.' As an old preacher once put it, "it's life - for a look!" This is what we meant earlier by saying 'something *must* happen to Jesus, and as a consequence, something *may* happen to us' - death happened to Jesus, but life can happen to us.

The faith that saves

At this point both the gospel and experience require we pause, and reflect a little on this word 'believe' used by Jesus. In the NT, faith assumes that in looking to Christ, we are looking away also from what put him on the cross - namely, our sin! The life of faith begins with a conscious decision to turn *from* sin, and *to* Christ; and continues, with the Spirit's help, as we do battle with sins that have become such learned behaviours that only 'warfare' can describe what will shift them (Galatians 5v17; 1 Peter 2v11).

But the NT also assumes that if we're looking to Jesus, we're also looking away from any personal merit we imagine might commend us to God. And so, if the summons to look away first addresses the wrong-doer, it also addresses the respectable right-doer, even the religious person; indeed, someone like Nicodemus! We see this portrayed perfectly in the parable of the Pharisee and Tax Collector (Luke 18v9-14). In that parable both go up to the temple to pray. The self-confident Pharisee begins,

'God, I thank you that I am not like other people-robbers, evildoers, adulterers, or even like this tax collector. I fast twice a week and give a tenth of all I get.' But the tax collector stood at a distance. He would not even look up to heaven, but beat his breast and said, 'God, have mercy on me, a sinner.'

Notice, whereas one looks to his imagined merits, the other looks solely to God's mercy. Even the word here for mercy is not the customary word in Greek, but another that means 'to cover;' a word synonymous with sacrifice, and used of Jesus' action (Hebrews 2v17) in atoning for the sins of his people. In asking for mercy the Tax Collector is looking to God to find grounds himself to forgive and restore. In the NT it's this faith that realised these blessings when focussed on the achievement of Jesus.

And so, when Jesus pressed the mysterious nature of the new birth, telling Nicodemus that, like the wind, it was outside our sphere of control, how do we imagine Nicodemus felt? I ask this because telling someone *'You must be born again'* but that only God can do it, doesn't seem a great evangelistic strategy! But actually, it wonderfully prepares Nicodemus for the essential prerequisite necessary to receiving new birth. It's as though Jesus is saying to Nicodemus: "New birth may not be something you can do, but I can! Therefore, Trust me." Stop trusting in yourself, your reputation, your good works - these things may give you credit before others - but only I can impart the life of the Spirit, eternal life! "Trust Me!"

As you see me, lifted up on the cross, bearing the world's sin, Nicodemus, trust me so your every sin may be forgiven. As you see me, raised-up from the dead, and into the Father's presence, trust me that you may know the gift of the Holy Spirit poured out upon you. Trust me! Come and be born again of water and Spirit, cleansed and empowered!

Earlier, I recalled an old preacher announcing it's 'Life for a look.' Maybe like me, you have known occasions when what you've looked at has moved you deeply. I recall early morning watches at sea, and the rising sun turning the water such a beautiful orange hue; I was transfixed. I have stood in Norway's mountains where the Northern Lights have lit up a winter night; and mornings where the sun turned ice in the air to a sparkling wonderland. My wife planted a small Acer tree in our back garden, and some mornings, I'm almost convinced, as the sun shines through its red leaves, that it's on fire. There is, however, another Son. And when we look to him in child-like trust, we are not only inspired but transformed. Faith in him releases power from him (Luke 8v44-46; Acts 3v12,16), that renews us, and we and our world are never the same again.

The faith that sustains

Another vital factor needs also to be considered. When the NT speaks of faith, it assumes not merely an attitude towards Christ, but incorporation into him. Faith so unites us with Christ, that an exchange takes place; not only does Jesus take our sin and discharge its debt, but we also have his obedience, and are accounted righteous. The apostle Paul puts it this way, *'God made him who had no sin to be sin for us so that in him we might become the righteousness of God'* (2 Corinthians 5v2). In another place, comparing the achievements of Adam and Jesus, he writes: *'just as through the disobedience of the one man the many were made sinners, so also through the obedience of the one man the many will be made righteous'* (Romans 5v19).

This wonderful truth is what enables the believer to withstand the accusations of the evil one, and his or her conscience. It's not unusual to hear salvation illustrated with the image of a school exercise book, in which are recorded, with big red crosses, all the errors we've made. These are the sins of our lives, but because of what Jesus has done, we are forgiven, and the pages are wiped clean. That, as far as it goes, is true; but it doesn't go far enough. For what Christ achieves in his life and death for us, is the book returned, the exercises completed, and all marked with big red ticks!

Earlier, in this week in which I'm writing, a young lady mailed me in despair. Something was close to driving her mad, and she just couldn't get past it (her words). Being young in the faith, she desperately wanted to please God, and so, was spending a lot of time 'praying.' Now prayer is a good thing, right? I mean, Jesus did it a lot; and taught his disciples to do it too. So prayer is a good thing, right? Wrong - if we're doing it, or any other religious exercise, to win acceptance or greater security before God. And so the young lady concludes, not surprisingly: "sometimes, I feel everything I think and do is failing his expectations."

What does the gospel say to such frustration? What should I say? I wrote the following; 'Now, about prayer. Do be careful! We can, as believers, start to obsess about things like prayer, imagining that the more we do it, the more secure in God's love we are. Of course, it applies to a lot of fundamentally good things. Remember, your prayer life is not where confidence before God is found; it's in Christ's prayer life. Not in your life performance as a Christian, but his life performance as your saviour. Not in your success over temptation, but in his.

Being 'in the right' with God begins and continues because of a righteousness that lies outside ourselves - it's in Jesus! I could begin praying now, and not stop until Christmas Day - I would be no more loved by God then than I (and you) are now! Isn't that incredible? Grace releases us to be everything we've been recreated to be. The purest prayer is just two words - "thank you!" Tim Keller wrote: "So the cross is both the place where God in the past paid the penalty for our sin and the place where believers in the present are encouraged by God's grace and inspired afresh by his love."

Now, this sounds almost too good to be true. My father used to say, "Kieran, remember, if something sounds too good to be true, it is!" Well, here is the exception that proves the rule. We might even think, if I'm accounted righteous because of what Jesus has done, I may as well just please myself! (Romans 6v1,15). Indeed! But what this confused conclusion overlooks is who this new 'self' is - someone in whom spirit has given birth to spirit, someone born of God.

A feature of this new work of God's grace, making sinners sons and daughters, is the profound display of God's love seen in its accomplishment. *'How great* (says John) *is the love the Father has lavished on us, that we should be called children of God!'* And that is what we are! (1 John 3v1). John talks like a man who never quite got over the display of God's grace present in his salvation. It's this love, visible at the cross, and poured into our hearts by the Holy Spirit, that accounts for the obedience that seeks not its advantage, but God's. (See Luke 7v36-50; 19v1-10).

And so, if an Israelite believed God's message (the good news of healing), he looked upon the lifted up serpent, and he was healed. If a man did not believe God's message, he did not look, and he died. Thus it is with us today: every man or woman must trust Christ to be healed, that is, consciously enter the life of the Spirit. It was this message of a crucified and risen saviour, and the promise of forgiveness and the Holy Spirit, that I quietly accepted in my bed-sit in Portsmouth, and that has become the solid bedrock for what was a very shaky life at the time. I would therefore encourage you to receive him too, and in doing so know God's forgiveness, and the power to be who you were always meant to be. He says, (Revelation 3v20 NIV), *'Here I am! I stand at the door and knock. If anyone hears my voice and opens the door, I will come in and eat with that person, and they with me.'*

6

The Signs of Life

We are now in a position to notice the most wonderful thing of all about the experience of New Birth; it works! By which I mean, it enables a thorough and effective new beginning in life. How many of us have sought to make life changes and pursue new and better goals, only to face defeat, and default all too quickly to who we've always been? This happens because the persons we've become, the behaviours learned, the habits cultivated and characters developed, don't just lay down helpless when we decide to change. Mere 'acts of will' cannot overturn what years of accumulated decision-making have already made us.

However, when we experience the new birth, what has happened is not just that we've resolved or decided to be different people, but that the Holy Spirit has formed in us instincts that inevitably produce change. To put it another way, it's not just that we start *making* different lifestyle choices, but that we *want* to.

In the first chapter, I shared how my grandmother would take me to the nearby stream to collect water each day. The truth is she didn't always have to walk to the stream for water but had permission to use the water pump in next door's garden. As time passed, the man of the house, for no reason other than that he could, withdrew his permission. And so, the daily trip to the stream took place right up until a new council house was occupied in the early 1960s with, wait for it, plumbed-in running water. Imagine the difference mains water made to the lives we lived there.

In another part of John's gospel, Jesus enters the temple precincts, the busy epicentre of Jewish religious life. In this setting, which had come to represent all that man thought he could do to experience God's approval, Jesus stood up and 'said in a loud voice... *"Whoever believes in me, as the Scripture has said, streams of living water will flow from within him."* Then John adds, *'By this he meant the Spirit, whom those who believed in him were later to receive'* (John 7v37-39). When a person is born again, the water of the Spirit is plumbed into the house! A new kind of life is begun!

It must now be clear that from a biblical and gospel perspective, a man or a woman cannot make themselves a Christian, only God can make a Christian. The Christianity Jesus is speaking of here, particularly in John 3, consists in what God does, and only in what we do as a new instinctual response to the new life God births in us. Do we see the difference? Living organisms don't only perform behaviours, they display signs of life.

To explore some of these 'signs of life,' J.I. Packer helpfully compares spiritual signs of life with the physical signs of life displayed in a newborn, to help us understand the experiential change of new birth. In the following, I borrow from Packer but add something of my own too. However, be assured, these signs aren't simply what religious imagination suggests, but the biblical account asserts.

Packer makes the point that there can be no more heart-wrenching experience than a mother giving birth to a still-born. And because this is so, at birth those present wait expectantly for the little one to show itself fully alive. What do they wait for? What are the signs that a new life has come into the world?

'First,' Packer reminds us, a 'baby cries instinctively; and the born-again Christian instinctively prays, crying to God in dependence, hope and trust as a child to his father,' (p.153).

Notice Packer stresses the 'instinctive' nature of the child's crying; it isn't performing a duty, but giving vent to what life has inclined and equipped it to do. And notice too, that the cry isn't yet with familiar words, or according to the rules of a received grammar. So too, the believer's cries in prayer are the *'wordless groans'* (Romans 8v26), that become the *'Abba Father'* (8v15) that the spirit moves the spiritually new-born to cry and testify to whose children they are.

If we ask why a newborn child cries, it's not merely an announcement to the world that it's here, but a cry to its mother, to be for him or her the life support it instinctively knows it needs. And of course, the child expects its needs to be met, and trusts they will be.

In one of his commentaries, Ben Witherington shares an experience he had while in Israel, that illustrates all the trust captured in that little Aramaic term for father or dad, 'Abba.' He tells of an occasion he was sitting reading on the end of a pier that extended out into the Sea of Galilee, and says: 'Intent on my reading, I was oblivious to my surroundings until I heard a young child's voice shouting, "Abba, Abba!" As I looked up, a five or six-year-old boy, face alight with a broad smile and eyes fixed upon the sole occupant of a fishing boat that had pulled up alongside the pier, was running the length of the dock at full speed. Then, without pausing, he leapt off the pier utterly abandoned to the confidence that he would be caught in the arms of his attentive Abba. The boatman was his Father!

The new-born of any culture may not be able to form the words, Father, Abba, or even dad, but the cries of the one born of the Spirit 'bear witness to the intimate relationship with God that is conveyed through the presence of the Holy Spirit,' (Witherington, 218), which begins with new birth.

Prayer is therefore a sign of spiritual life. And in the same way that when a newborn fails to cry, it suggests something's wrong, so it is for the believer with prayer. It's not that a duty has been left unmet, but one of the vital signs of life is absent. On reflection, I find it significant that the young man who shared the gospel with me, also knew he had to bring me into the presence of the father, in prayer. He illustrated to me that being a Christian isn't only about beliefs I must accept, but a father I must embrace. One who, when we turn to him, is waiting and watching, and then upon seeing us, runs to embrace us. Prayer is what the one embraced, wants to say in response.

Secondly, Packer reminds us, the 'baby sucks instinctively, and the born-again person also feels a hunger for spiritual food, first the milk, and then the meat of God's revealed word,' (p.154).

As any new parent will tell us, once the newborn has displayed the first sign of life by crying, the next sign that all is well is its wish to feed. And again, the need to do this is present from the very start in the sucking action that children are born with. It's a response that can need stimulating by introducing the child to its mother for milk, but it soon shows that it's there. The need to be fed is therefore not just a behaviour one learns, but a sign that life is present, and all is well. And this need for feeding and the growth it inevitably leads to can become an issue, as the little one develops. I recall the weekly visits by the nurse to weigh our eldest daughter, and waiting with bated breath to hear the news she was a little heavier.

This need for food is also a sign of life in the spiritually newborn. In the Apostle Peter's first letter, he reminds

Christian's they were 'born again... through the living and enduring word of God,' and then tells them, 'Like newborn babies, crave pure spiritual milk, so that by it you may grow up in your salvation, now that you have tasted that the Lord is good,' (1 Peter 2v2-3).

Notice again the believer's feeding is not simply a duty, but something the born-again are expected to crave, and encouraged to, in the same way, a midwife encourages what should be natural to a child. A child's feeding also develops with the child; eventually, an exclusive milk diet must give way to more solid food that provides the nourishment equal to their more demanding lives. In another place, the bible laments those who 'still need milk and not solid food, which is for the mature,' (Hebrews 5v12-14).

A born again believer cannot help but desire the milk of God's word. One of the first acts I remember in my journey to understand what had happened to me that night of encounter was to purchase a bible. I had no idea about the varied translations, and so bought an old King James Version. Its archaic expressions didn't always make understanding easy, but as an awkward wrapper on chocolate I was eager to eat, I persevered and was richly blessed in the consumption. A newborn believer would probably benefit more from a modern, but faithful translation, like the ESV or NIV, although the NLT also has its merits. All the while, the exercise is one of hearing the father speak, to comfort, encourage, and challenge us from his 'living word.'

Thirdly, Packer reminds us, a 'baby moves, turning its head, flexing its limbs, later on rolling, crawling, tottering, toddling, exploring; and similarly, the newborn person moves in the spiritual realm...' (p.154).

The reference here is clearly to both the newborn, and toddler. As my pupils back at school discovered, living things

move. It is an undeniable sign of life; even less sophisticated
life. Children at the primary school level are often shocked by
experiments that show the extent to which a humble plant's
roots and leaves will travel to get water and light.

So too, the born again Christian; he or she is active in
the things of God. That activity begins with obedience to his
word, keeping the relationship personal. But every Christian
becomes 'zealous for good deeds.' As a spiritual newborn the
emphasis in activity is often around learning about God, and
his purposes in Christ, in the kingdom, and in the world. But
as that foundation gets laid, it becomes increasingly clear that
we are to align our lives with those purposes. In Paul's letter
to Ephesus, he reminds believers, *'we are God's handiwork,
created in Christ Jesus to do good works, which God prepared
in advance for us to do,'* (2v10).

The point here is that whatever God's purposes in the
church and the world are, we are called to play our part in them.
That call will always be to *'live in accordance with the Spirit
(and) have our minds set on what the Spirit desires,'* (Romans
8v5); but it will also be a call to play our part, employing
'gifts' the Spirit has given us. There is both a challenge and
an exhilaration in 'moving' as a spirit-born believer. We will
often be called to resist the pressures around us to conform,
and yet also align ourselves and gifts with the most powerful
and enduring dynamic on earth - the kingdom of God.

Fourthly, a baby often tends to resemble its parents; so
too the born again believer. He or she quickly demonstrate
a likeness to their father and other siblings. Every parent
knows just how quickly others start to notice this likeness.
Often it's in the eyes or facial expression, but as a child grows,
the similarities can be striking, from simple mannerisms to
full-blown personality traits.

In the physical realm, we put this down to inheritance;
we pass on DNA from one generation to another, and so

inevitably, family likenesses emerge. With those born again, inheritance also plays its part, as the Spirit births in us a resemblance to Jesus. Indeed, the Holy Spirit is called both the 'Spirit of God' and the 'Spirit of Christ' in the scriptures.

Again, while in the physical realm we play a part in reproducing attitudes and behaviours we see in our parents, the much more fundamental truth is that they are to some mysterious extent, within us too. The apostle Paul refers to this very truth at work in the spiritual realm: *'And we all, who with unveiled faces contemplate the Lord's glory, are being transformed into his image with ever-increasing glory, which comes from the Lord, who is the Spirit,'* (2 Corinthians 3v18). Notice, the born again contemplate the Lord, in the way a child would its parents, but who both become is what their genetic, or spiritual inheritance, enables them to.

We see the extent to which this was the common understanding of the biblical authors by their approach to ethical living. That approach can be stated by the simple injunction, "Be who you are!" John, in his letters, makes the point that a believer will not continue sinning, as a lifestyle choice. Why? Because 'they have been born of God.'

Fifthly, Packer reminds us that a 'baby rests, relaxing completely and sleeping soundly in adult arms and wherever else feels firm; and in the same way, the born-again person rests in the knowledge that God's everlasting arms are underneath him,' (p.154-5). Packer appropriately quotes Psalm 131v2, *'I have calmed and quieted myself, I am like a weaned child with its mother; like a weaned child I am content.'*

This 'rest' is the byproduct of the Spirit at work in the hearts of the born-again. The first fruits of the Spirit that the apostle draws our attention to are *'love, joy and peace.'* It's God's love that the Spirit pours into Christian hearts; it's the joy of the Lord that the Spirit makes real in Christian lives;

and it's the peace Christ leaves with us, that the Spirit enables to become the rest that quietens the believing soul in every trying circumstance.

Here then are 'the signs of life.' The born again person is not merely one who has decided to become a Christian, but one into whose life the Holy Spirit has come. Having arrived, he births into that life the instinct to speak to the father, to hear from the father, be active in the business of the father, reflect something of a likeness to the father, and rest unreservedly in the faithfulness of the father.

7

The Family of the Firstborn

I wonder, have you ever been mistaken for someone else? Once, when my wife and I were travelling in the North of England, we decided to visit a transport museum local to where we were staying. We'd had a great morning looking at the various exhibits and come lunchtime, set off for the restaurant and found a table. After our meal, my wife headed for the restroom, as our American cousins call it. She wasn't gone long when a lady came over to our table and, to my surprise, sat down beside me. Leaning towards me, in a conspiratorial kind of way, she whispered, "You're that man who plays ****** on television, aren't you?" Now, of course, I wasn't, but I so wanted to say "yes!" It was clear she was a big fan, and even a momentary dose of misplaced adulation would have gone down well, but I resisted. The poor lady, sadly, walked back to her seat; neither of us satisfied with the outcome.

The Root of Christlikeness

In Scripture it's clear, God's wish is that Christians come to resemble his Son. Jesus himself was 'the image of the invisible God, the firstborn over all creation' (Colossians 1v15), but so too, *'those God foreknew he also predestined to be conformed to the image of his Son, that he might be the firstborn among many brothers and sisters'* (Romans 8v29). In this, we see that Christians coming to resemble Jesus has always been the divine intention, and the consequence of family connection - he is *'the firstborn among many brothers and sisters.'*

Having said this, we must not assume the believer has no part to play in growing to resemble their elder brother; the opposite is true. For NT writers, we make what God is doing in us a living reality by understanding how it proceeds, and applying conscious effort to the same end. The believer knows you *'work out your salvation with fear and trembling, for it is God who works in you to will and to act in order to fulfil his good purpose,'* (Philippians 2v12). We work because God is already at work. The call is to *'the obedience that comes from faith'* (Romans 1v5). Growing to become more like Jesus is no mere consequence of determined religious effort, but begins with realising what God in Christ has done *for* us, is doing *in* us, and wants to do *with* us. To see this dynamic at work, we will draw on Paul's sustained treatment of faith generated obedience in Romans 6.

The Branches of Christlikeness

It's not unusual in Christian writings to find those who claim getting to grips with Romans 6 was a defining moment on their journey. My first brush with the power of its truth came in Watchman Nee's *'The Normal Christian Life'* many years ago. Later, Martyn Lloyd Jones in his exposition of Romans 6, *'The New Man'* did the very same for me. More recently, Jerry Bridges, in one of his books, refers to Paul's frequent doxologies of praise and, as he writes on the truth of Romans 6, admits, "this is the way I feel in my heart right now as I write."

So, what is Romans 6 about? Up to this point in his letter, Paul has been dealing with how, through the cross, God has released sinners from *the penalty of sin*. Now in chapter 6, he starts explaining how, through the believer's co-crucifixion and co-resurrection with Jesus, they have been released from *the reigning power of sin*, so that they *'too may live a new life* (6v4).' It's this transformation, when embraced by faith, and acted upon in life, that makes us more like Jesus. To reflect on ch.6v1-14 it may help to think of *facts* we should know (v1-10), a situation we should *reckon* upon (v11-12), and an *offering* we should make (13-14).

The Facts we should Know...

Paul responds, with a resounding negative, to those who think the display of God's free grace in the gospel means they have the freedom to sin (v1). He won't even contemplate the idea. If we ask why, it's because, as he says (v2), 'We... *have died to sin.*' If we ask how we have died to sin, it's because, (v3), '*all of us who were baptised into Christ Jesus were baptised into his death.*' And he adds (v4), '*just as Christ was raised from the dead through the glory of the Father, we too may live a new life.*' The bottom line is this: Christ died and rose again, and the believer has also in some sense, died to sin and risen to new life, as a consequence of their relationship to him.

Before examining what dying to sin and being able to live a new life means, it will help to reflect on how the NT portrays the believer's relationship to Christ, which is that of *union with him.* We see it clearly in (v5) of this passage: Paul writes, '*if we have been united with him in a death like his, we will certainly also be united with him in a resurrection like his.*' But what is it to be '*united with him*'?

Paul in this letter sees that union in two respects. First, there is a representative union in which the merits, or otherwise, of the representative figure accrue to those he represents. In ch. 5v12-21, just such a union is understood between Adam and the whole human race. He acted as our representative before God, but having failed, brought himself and us all into condemnation. Christ, however, represented a people too. In discharging their responsibilities successfully before God, righteousness accrues to them, that in the gospel offer is received by faith. It is the truth of this union that makes the gospel the good news it is. It explains how, despite their failings, a believer can nevertheless have confidence before God, and know that *there is therefore now no condemnation to those who are in Christ Jesus*. As Bridges puts it: 'just as Adam's sin was as truly our sin, as if we had committed it, so Christ's perfect obedience to God's law and his death to pay the penalty of a broken law is just as much our obedience and death, as if we had perfectly obeyed God's law and died on that cross.'

This, however, brings us to a second sense in which the believer is in union with Christ. Not only is it a union that overturns *my guilty verdict*, but one that overturns *the reigning power* of sin in me, enabling growth in Christlikeness. So it isn't only a union in which Christ does something *for* me, but a vital and spiritual union in which Jesus, through his death and resurrection – does something *in* me. As to what that is, Paul begins again (v6): *'For we know that our old self was crucified with him so that the body ruled by sin might be done away with.'* That *old self*, who we once were in Adam, and under condemnation, has died at the cross. But notice, that death was *so that* the body ruled by sin might be done away with. In other words, the body in which we were once helpless slaves to sin - that body has been done away with, and that tyranny broken. But something else has happened too - due to our spiritual union with the Christ who also rose, *'we too may live a new life'* (v7). Now, it's true that because of Christ's resurrection the believer will rise on the last day, but Paul is saying more than that here. He's saying that because of Christ's resurrection, we too (v13), *'have been brought from death to life'* - now!

The truth is that when a person believes, they become united to Christ in such a way that not only does his representation on their behalf change their legal status, but through vital, spiritual union with him, *change the people they become*. It can therefore be seen why 'baptism' is such an eloquent initiatory rite, reflecting as it does not only on the public identification of a believer with Christ, but their incorporation into him, and by extension, into the benefits of his death, burial, and his resurrection.

Now, what did Paul expect those at Rome to do with this truth of their union with Christ? We must ask this, because, although it's true, making its truth impact the lives they lived required something more.

The Situation we should reckon...

Paul continues, *'In the same way, count yourselves dead to sin but alive to God in Christ Jesus,'* (v11). This verse is more significant than its length suggests. Earlier we noted that discovering God's power a reality in our daily lives involves exercising faith. This is Paul saying the same thing. In the King James Version of the bible the verse reads, *'Likewise reckon ye also yourselves to be dead indeed unto sin, but alive unto God through Jesus Christ our Lord.'* What the NIV asks us to *'count'* the KJV asks us to *'reckon'*. Both words translate the word, *'logizomai'*, which comes from the world of finance and means, 'to calculate, or take into account.'

What Paul is encouraging may be illustrated by our activity when making a purchase of some kind. When we shop for everyday items, we generally pay by cash or card. Although we may seldom think about it, when using a card we assume the money is in the bank. The strength of the assumption is rarely tested - until a card is rejected, and a look of surprise comes across our faces. However, if we are purchasing something substantial, we sensibly take care that the funds are available, and so avoid the unpleasantness of surprise. Paul, by the truth of our vital union with Christ who died and rose, has shown that the body once ruled by sin has been done away with, and as new creations, we are now able to live the new life God has called and equipped us to live.

Count upon it, says Paul. Start factoring this in. Take it into account. Remember who you now are.

Now the importance of this point cannot be overstated. It's important because it's true, but also because as basic human psychology shows, our behaviours are our beliefs writ large - beliefs about ourselves, other people, the world around us; even God himself. These beliefs determine what we come to expect of ourselves, and therefore, what we're therefore willing to attempt. The gospel, however, overwrites these old, false assumptions in a powerful, transformative way. First, it demonstrates how profoundly we are loved, for *'God demonstrates his own love for us in this: While we were still sinners, Christ died for us'* (Romans 5v8). Secondly, it announces that in Christ's death we too have died, both to the penalty and reigning power of sin. Truly, the lives in which sin was once master, are behind us. Thirdly, it reminds us that we *'have been brought from death to life,'* (6v13), and so *'may live a new life'* (6v4). Paul wants us to consciously reckon upon this exercise of God's power in us - the same as the mighty strength he exerted when he raised Christ from the dead' (Ephesians 1v19-20).

The Offering we should make...

Given what Paul has taught us about our union with Christ, there seems only one reasonable response: *'Do not offer any part of yourself to sin as an instrument of wickedness, but offer yourselves to God as those who have been brought from death to life; and offer every part of yourself to him as an instrument of righteousness'* (Romans 6v13). The Christian is to offer their entire selves to God, or as Tom Schreiner puts it, 'believers must consciously choose to place themselves at the disposal of their master, Lord, and king' (2018; p.325). Some scholars see a military association in these words, and the image is helpful as the verb tenses suggest both a once and for all decisive action, just as when one enlists in an army; but also an ongoing, habitual action, as when the enlisted turn-to daily to hear their Captain's orders and obey.

The Fruit of Christlikeness

Having considered the root of Christlikeness - family connection with Jesus; and the branches - the believer's union, or co-crucifixion and co-resurrection with Christ; we will now reflect briefly on the fruit or the three most fundamental orientations of the Christlike life. We see these orientations present in the opening scenes of the gospel record, suggesting their foundational significance for both Jesus and his followers.

An attitude to sin

At the beginning of Jesus's public ministry, he was led into the wilderness and subjected to severe temptation by the devil, (Matthew 4v1-11; Mark 1v12-13; Luke 4v1-13). Despite unique elements, given who he was, it's clear this exchange is to some extent paradigmatic for every believer's battle with sin. In all sin, we succumb to the invitation not to trust God, and adhere to the beneficial and loving limits he has placed upon us, but pursue our imagined advantage in some other way. We see this dynamic throughout the bible, with Adam and Eve in the garden, Israel in the wilderness, and indeed the wayward son in the Lord's parable. The same dynamic is implied in the very words the bible uses for sin, expressing rebellion against God in either missing the mark, or transgressing his boundaries, and the inevitable emptiness and alienation that sin always leads to (1 John 3v4; Luke 15v16-17; Lane, 2013, 69).

So, how did Jesus handle these temptations? He refused to distrust his father, and so must we. Success in battling with sin begins not in how we look at it, but how we look at the father. When we look at him and remind ourselves afresh of his costly love for us (Romans 5v8; 1 John 4v10), we also see sin for what it truly is; not some technical breach of divine/ human relations, but a slap on the face of the one who's love for us exceeds all others. It's not a mystery that the hardest people to hurt are those who love us. If we ask where that attitude renews itself hourly and daily, it's in the gospel and at the cross, that moves us to cry, *'See what great love the father has lavished on us, that we should be called children of God! And that is what we are!'* (1 John 3v1).

Next, Christ handled temptation with a determined refusal to exceed the beneficial and loving limits God had placed upon him. We hear this resolve in his response to the devil, *"Away from me, Satan"* (Matthew 4v10); and see it present in the believer's refusal to *'offer any part of yourself to sin as an instrument of wickedness'* (Romans 6v13). In the latter's case, while we know sin no longer reigns, we soon discover it remains to persist in resisting our efforts towards obedience (see Luke 4v13). In light of this, the Apostle reminds believers they must *'by the Spirit ...put to death the misdeeds of the body'* (Romans 8v13); or in conscious dependence upon the Holy Spirit, strive to deprive sin of the conditions that allow it to thrive.

In the accounts of Christ's temptations, his final response is a refusal again to seek an imagined advantage other than God's will and way. To the devil, the response is always, *'it is written'* (Mark 4v4,7,10). This attitude to sin will be seen too in all who would follow Jesus, and so we turn next to Christ's orientation towards the Father.

An orientation to God

An unmistakable feature of Christ's life was that he consciously took God's Word as his manifesto. In Luke 4, after baptism, the same Spirit who just sustained him in temptation brings him to the synagogue in Nazareth. Here, where he once heard his father Joseph's voice, he and others hear the Heavenly Father speak. The theme is the Servant of the Lord which Jesus reads (Luke 4v18-19),

> *"The Spirit of the Lord is on me,*
> *because he has anointed me*
> *to proclaim good news to the poor.*
> *He has sent me to proclaim freedom for the*
> *prisoners and recovery of sight for the blind,*
> *to set the oppressed free, to proclaim the*
> *year of the Lord's favour."*

Having read these words, he handed back the scroll, and conscious of all eyes upon him announces *"Today this scripture is fulfilled in your hearing"* (4v20). By doing what Jesus has just done, he is identifying with God's promised end-time deliverer in Isaiah. However, the issue is not only one of identity, but ministry. He is the Servant of the Lord who exercises his role on behalf of the father (Isaiah 42v1; 52v13) and for the benefit of his people (53v4-6). At Nazareth, the story of God's redemptive purpose is identified and calibrated with for all to hear and see.

It's this alignment of life, in word and action, with the same father's purposes, that makes for Christlikeness in a follower of Jesus. Jesus said to his disciples, *"If you keep my commands, you will remain in my love, just as I have kept my fathers commands and remain in his love"* (John 15v10). These commands are the practical outworking of God's purposes, recorded in the bible, informing every believer's identity and calling. As Jesus took a very clear lead from Scripture, so the believer's calling is not to fit loosely, but align precisely with what God has done in the past (OT), is doing in the present, and will do in the future (NT).

The believer's orientation to God is visible in four life-long habits. First, in the daily reading of scripture, the believer grows to become more familiar with God and his purposes in the world and for his people. Secondly, they listen to the voice of God as the Spirit sensitises to the personal need for change in old patterns of thought and behaviour. Thirdly, the believer brings these convictions prayerfully to God in confession, asking also for the Spirit's help with change. Fourthly, the believer makes whatever life adjustments 'keeping in step with the Spirit' requires of them (Galatians 5v25). It's this continuing dynamic of life engagement with the Word and Spirit that extends out also beyond everyday obedience into sensing the particular calling of God upon our life; callings that personal gifting anticipates and equips us for, (Romans 12v6).

Responsibility to others

In our previous consideration of Christ's and therefore his follower's orientation to the father, we thought not only of personal obedience but our place in God's wider purposes. Jesus *always* did what pleased the father, but he also came, not to be served, but to serve, and give his life a ransom for others (Mark 10v45). It is remarkable but true that Christ's calling was to please the father, by serving others. It's also remarkable but true that the believer's calling is to please the Father by serving others. The question must therefore be, how did Christ, and now the believer, do this?

Throughout Christ's earthly ministry we find him responding to the practical needs of others, sometimes in the provision of pressing bodily needs, or with miraculous healings and deliverance from spiritual oppression. Of course, ultimately, the deliverance was from sin's curse and by means of his death, the provision of forgiveness and new life in the Spirit. While no follower of Christ can match this, or needs to, they can nevertheless witness to the availability of these great transforming gifts. It's clear Jesus had such a witness in mind when he told the disciples that *'the forgiveness of sins will be preached in his name to all nations,'* and then said, *'you are witnesses of these things,'* (Luke 24v47-48).

Every believer is called to be a witness to Jesus Christ. This can sound like a daunting responsibility, and so a few words of encouragement may be in order. First, the task begins with the prayerful offer of ourselves to God. It is he who ultimately convicts and calls others to himself. Secondly, our growing awareness of the gospel in content and application is always preparing us for that occasion when someone asks us to *'give a reason for the hope that you have,'* (1 Peter 3v15). Thirdly, a witness does not commend themselves, but another. Feelings of personal inadequacy, while understandable, is irrelevant to the exercise as it's Christ's adequacy we're commending. One of the world's greatest witnesses admitted that when he turned up to share the gospel at Corinth, *'I came to you in weakness with great fear and trembling,'* (1 Corinthians 2v3). Finally, our call to witness is as part of a local family of faith, the church. As it seeks to bring the message of redeeming love to that part of the fallen world in which God has placed it, we can all play a part, however minor we might feel it to be. As I reflect on the young man brave enough to share the gospel with me, and what coming to know Christ because of him has meant for me, I cannot help but feel gratitude. The call for me now is to make someone else grateful.

8

Our Future Hope

At the time of writing, I have now been without my mother for just under a year. I got the call from my father early one morning to say she'd had a stroke and was taken to hospital. In a very broken voice, he added, "It doesn't look good, son." The events that led to the call began the previous evening. My mother had been at the back of the house with a brush, on her latest campaign in a life-long battle with dust and dirt. She made it into the greenhouse and, it seems, fell into some soft soil, not to rise again in her own strength. My father waited, wondering why it was taking her so long to come back indoors. His discovery lies heavily in his memory, for try as he did, he could not revive her. Two days later she left us.

It is not easy to write what I just have, but of course, many, many people, nearly all of us at some time, have known the pain of loved ones wrenched from us. And always, where love has been the cement binding us, it's as though something of our very selves has been ripped away. But one question is surely worth asking, "Where is she now?" If I were a strict materialist, my worldview would oblige me to reject any notion of her continuing existence, other than in the memories of those who knew her.

What makes one detail of my mother's passing significant, particularly for my father, is that about a year before she died, on an earlier campaign, she also made it into the greenhouse and fell in almost the very same place. When my father found

her she was out-cold. Although he managed to revive her, to
his astonishment she was angry with him. She wanted to 'go
back' to where she had just been; "full of vivid colour, bright
with light; where she felt good and always wanted to be." And
so, she protested, "Let me go back!"

Now, what am I to make of this? My father, on the day
in question, was in no doubt it was some kind of heavenly
experience. When I ponder what my mother insisted was
real, I'm challenged. From the perspective of the gospels,
transit between this life and the next is decidedly one-way.
On the narrow road, to which Jesus is the gate, one is not
conscious of returning traffic. In another place, (Luke 16v26
NIV), he tells an unhappy man wanting to return, *'between us
and you a great chasm has been set in place, so that those who
want to go from here to you cannot, nor can anyone cross over
from there to us.'* Although a parable, it seems unlikely the
comment bears no relation to the realities of the situation.
Accounts like my mother's, often dismissed as mere tricks
of the brain as it copes with deprivation of vital oxygen, still
tantalise us, like postcards from some exotic land the visitor
reached but was refused entry. So, what can be said about
the life to come, that builds on the more solid foundation of
biblical evidence, and warrant's acceptance?

Personal Future Hope

First, Jesus Christ came back from the dead.

We have already explored some of the grounds for believing
this, and repetition seems unnecessary. According to the
accounts, Jesus did die, and it's on the firm presupposition
of this death, that his resurrection in the NT is advanced.
There is simply no suggestion whatever, from the range of
interested parties, that anything less than death took place.

But Jesus is nevertheless reported as having come back from the dead. It's true that some of the evidence is circumstantial, but along with the reported eyewitness accounts, the cumulative case is strong. If any other reported feat was under review - say that Jesus could regularly jump from a standing position to a height of say 10 metres - the range in number, variety, timing and location of witnesses would oblige us to take the report seriously. We may argue that's different, some have already jumped quite high, (Rune Almén jumped 1.90 m in 1980), but we would be missing the point. In history, it's the accounts of those present that give an event its credibility. We could of course decide the witnesses themselves were suspect, but nothing in the record obliges us to take this view; quite the opposite.

Secondly, Jesus said he would rise, and others would too.

On at least three occasions, in the course of his ministry Jesus told the disciples, *'the Son of Man... must be killed and after three days rise again,'* (Mark 8v31, 9v31, 10v34). Predicting accurately his resurrection, bodes well for followers of Jesus to whom he made a similar promise. Speaking of his father's house, where he was going to prepare a place for them, he promises, *'Because I live, you also will live,'* (John 14v19). In (11v25) of the same gospel, Jesus makes an earlier breathtaking promise, *'I am the resurrection and the life. The one who believes in me will live, even though they die; and whoever lives by believing in me will never die.'* The confidence followers of Jesus can therefore have in their resurrection is supported by two pillars; the promised resurrection of Christ that eyewitnesses tell us took place, and the further promise, that those who believe in him will also rise.

Thirdly, believers experience a spiritual resurrection first, then a physical

In the encounter between Jesus and Nicodemus, we saw that while from the human side *faith* secures eternal life, from the divine side, *Spirit gives birth to spirit.* Beale suggests Ezekiel 36 which underpins the exchange with Nicodemus, is 'virtually equivalent to the prediction of resurrection by the Spirit' in Ezekiel 37 (2011; p.678). That chapter, in which dead bones are made alive as the Spirit breathes into them, anticipates Jesus breathing upon his disciples (John 20v22) and saying, "Receive the Holy Spirit." Reflecting on Romans 6, Packer (2005, 89) refers to the believer's spiritual experience of co-resurrection with Jesus - she is one in whom the power that wrought Jesus resurrection is now at work... the spiritually risen person.

Now, why is the believer's experience of the Spirit vital to a doctrine like the resurrection of the body? Because, in a way that's ultimately a mystery, the presence of the Spirit is, (Ephesians 1v14), '*a deposit guaranteeing our inheritance until the redemption of those who are God's possession.*' The Spirit is a 'down payment,' or the first instalment of an amount due, as it was and is in the world of commerce. Used here metaphorically, Paul is saying that the presence of the Holy Spirit is an assurance of our full inheritance, but more - he is something of what is to come, present with us already.

Another sense in which the presence of the Spirit impacts future physical resurrection is that of agency. In Romans 8v11(ESV) we read, '*If the Spirit of him who raised Jesus from the dead dwells in you, he who raised Christ Jesus from the dead will also give life to your mortal bodies through his Spirit who dwells in you.*' If God by his Spirit raised Jesus, he will by his Spirit raise our mortal bodies too. And why will it happen for us? Simply this, because his Spirit '*dwells in you.*'

When we contemplate what our physical bodies are reduced to postmortem, it's understandably hard to imagine that anything new could come of them; certainly anything of our previous selves that occupied them. However, the presence of the Spirit adds to the assurance of Christ's resurrection, and the promise of our own, by taking us back to creation itself when the Spirit of God was first 'hovering over the waters,' then breathed into lifeless Adam; the first, which was 'formless, empty and dark,' came to teem with life, whilst the second became a living soul.

Fourthly, believers experience bodily resurrection.

As Jesus said (John 14v19), *'because I live, you also will live.'* There was a physicality about the resurrected body of the Lord Jesus; indeed, Thomas was able to place his hand upon him; and the disciples enjoy eating with him. It is this hope, regarding ourselves that is in view when the NT (Romans 8v23) talks of *'the redemption of our bodies.'* Before however, we consider our own resurrected state, we will be better served by seeing it in relation to the whole sweep of Christian future hope.

Full Christian Hope

The wider biblical testimony suggests certain characteristics of what the apostle calls *'the glory to be revealed.'*

The first point to be made is that the glory anticipated far exceeds what we presently know. As the apostle says (1 Corinthians 2v9) *'What no eye has seen, what no ear has heard, and what no human mind has conceived - the things God has prepared for those who love him.'* However, the extent of what lies ahead is captured first by Jesus, then Peter, as *'the renewal'* (Matthew 19v28), or *'final restoration of all things'* (Acts 3v21 NLT). Truly, what is to come is of cosmic proportions. Nevertheless, as Paul says, (1 Corinthians 2v10) the Spirit has revealed certain things to us.

A New Environment

'The reality,' says Milne (1998; p.338), 'towards which all God's purposes are moving is called, *'a new heaven and a new earth'*' (Isaiah 65v17; 66v22; 2 Peter 3v13). This new environment will be free from the present world's 'bondage to decay' which reduces all organic life to a battle for survival. Truly, the last enemy, death - in all its forms - defeated at the cross, will be routed forever. As John (Revelation 21) tells us *'death shall be no more.'* The same thought is present in the description of the new heavens and earth having *'no longer any sea.'* To ancient peoples the sea often represented 'the threat of evil and tribulation' (Beale, p.466), being typically the place where one's enemies approached, and tyranny began. But, no more!

In place of all that mars and corrupts our present environment, we find in the new heavens and new earth, a rich source of life and renewal:

'Then the angel showed me the river of the water of life, as clear as crystal, flowing from the throne of God and of the Lamb down the middle of the great street of the city. On each side of the river stood the tree of life, bearing twelve crops of fruit, yielding its fruit every month. And the leaves of the tree are for the healing of the nations.' (Revelation 22v1-2)

There are two points to notice here. First, instead of forces at work to destroy, God is at work 'restoring fulness of life to the world' (Benyon, 2010, p.70). Consequently, those who live in this environment are never without what will enable life to flourish. The healing leaves of the tree of life, depict again the reversal of corruption we associate with our fallen circumstance presently, and so not surprisingly the writer continues, (v3) *'No longer will there be any curse.'*

It's hard for us to imagine living in an environment that isn't to some degree hostile to life. As I write, we're just emerging from our third lockdown in a year, in an attempt to curb the destructive effects of a pandemic that has already taken tens of thousands of lives in the UK, and millions of lives worldwide. Behind these figures lies the pain of families who've lost loved ones; people who've lost their jobs; and the insecurity that descends on family life as a consequence. The present crisis has confronted many of us with fragility and vulnerability in life that we always knew was there, but managed to avoid. In the new environment, where *all* things have been made new, old enemies like disease and death no longer threaten.

A New Physical Body

So, who lives in this renewed environment? As we saw, it is 'the redemption of our bodies' that expresses the future, personal hope of believers; but what will those bodies be like? Jesus, in his resurrection, is called (1 Corinthians 15v23) *'the first fruits'* in distinction from 'those who belong to him' but with him constitute the full harvest. Given this common identity between Christ and his own, many have seen his resurrection as modelling our own. There was certainly a physicality about the risen Christ; he could be touched, and dined with, and so will we. He was identifiable by those who met him, and so too will we. In Mark 12v24 we read that *'the dead rise.'* Says Milne (2002, p.137), the implication here is of 'self-conscious personal identity after death. The same 'selves' who passed into death will emerge beyond it.'

Having said this, it's clear from 1 Corinthians 15, Paul's fullest discussion of bodily resurrection, that our resurrection bodies will display characteristics discontinuous with who we have previously been. Paul says 'The body that is sown is perishable, it is raised imperishable; it is sown in dishonour, it is raised in glory; it is sown in weakness, it is raised in power; it is sown a natural body, it is raised a spiritual body.' In other words, our resurrection bodies will not be given to ageing or decay; but possess an excellence about them; they, it seems, will exhibit physical, rational and spiritual powers not presently known by us; and be utterly attuned to their original intention of living in communion with God. In John's first letter he says, *'we know that when Christ appears, we shall be like him, for we shall see him as he is,'* (3v2). The context of these words suggests a moral and ethical purity, once lost to us, but natural once again.

What about the activities that will occupy our renewed bodies? It is inconceivable that our bodies will not find activities equal to their renewed capacities. We might therefore reasonably assume that there will be physical, rational and spiritual challenges made of us. Picking up on the imagery of the book of Revelation, Grudem suggests, 'we might imagine that both musical and artistic activities would be done to the glory of God. Perhaps people will work at the whole range of investigation and development of the creation by technological, creative, and inventive means, thus exhibiting the full extent of their excellent creation in the image of God (1994; p. 1162). What will characterise our lives in the new heavens and new earth will undoubtedly be that of satisfaction, fulfilment and at last, a sense that 'I was made for this!'

A New Experience of each other

A further, unmistakable truth about the glory yet to be revealed is that we enjoy it - together. Stated simply, heaven is a social experience. 'All the bible's pictures of the life of the heavenly world are corporate,' writes Bruce Milne, It is seen as a perfect city (Hebrews 13v14), as a victorious kingdom (Hebrews 12v28), as a holy temple (Ezekiel 40-48), and as a wedding feast (Revelation 19v7). That final image of a feast reminds us again of the feast the father throws to celebrate the return of his erring son. But what is it about feasts? They are occasions that celebrate togetherness! Heaven is one great, un-ending celebration of togetherness.

Earthly relationships can be the most rewarding and fulfilling of all the experiences we enjoy. The presence of sin can of course transform them into the most destructive of experiences, but the truth is that when all is well, family and friends are the means of bringing us untold pleasure. However, in the glory, undreamed of possibilities at the level of social relationships lie before us.

To begin, it's reasonable to assume that we will recognise one another in the new heavens and new earth. Our own 'selves' are raised, and will surely be as recognisable as Christ's self when Mary cried out in recognition of him (John 20v16). But will we recognise those who were dearest to us? Our Lord's words about 'no giving or taking in marriage' might suggest not. But that is surely to miss the Lord's point. An absence of marriage, as we now know it, doesn't mean a lessening of love, as we will then know it. On the grounds of some continuity with what we now experience, Milne suggests, 'a surviving awareness of specialness and belonging.' And even where that might not be present, love will reign supreme. Now, how can we make such a statement without danger of contradiction? Our final reflection explains...

A New Experience of God

One of the most beautiful scenes in scripture is of our great grandparents in the garden at the beginning. Not only was everything present to satisfy earthly and physical appetites, but so too was God. He enters early into conversation with the couple and, while later walking in the garden in the cool of the day notices their absence and calls out to them. This scene speaks of loving concern and intimacy. Sin of course destroyed that intimacy, but not forever. And so, if our bibles were written on one long scroll, and its ends brought to meet each other, we discover that God is back in the garden again. 'Look!' shouts a loud voice, (Revelation 21v3) 'God's dwelling place is now among his people, and he will dwell with them.'

It seems almost unbelievable, but (changing the metaphor) 'God and the Lamb (Jesus) will be in the city;' and so familiar will they be to its inhabitants, says John, (v4), 'they will see his face.' To our present fallen selves, the thought of God's presence can seem threatening. We called our eldest daughter, Jessica, which in Hebrew means 'God is looking.' When I first shared this with her, she cowered; the thought was not altogether welcome. But is it not a great thing to have this misperception corrected by Jesus, and hear (Luke 15v20) that while the prodigal was still 'a long way off, his father saw him and was filled with compassion for him; he ran to his son, threw his arms around him and kissed him.' As this story reflects on the joy of heaven at the return of the lost, we simply cannot imagine that life later, in the new heaven and earth, will be anything less.

Indeed, just as in the parable of the restored son (Luke 15), the first display of emotion and reckless abandon gives way to a feast, so in Revelation 19v7 we also read, 'Let us rejoice and be glad and give him glory! For the wedding of the

Lamb has come, and his bride has made herself ready.' In the story of the returning son, the best animal the father owns is sacrificed to celebrate the return, and cement the family's reunion. John, in Revelation (19v9), tells us, *'Then the angel said to me, "Write this: Blessed are those who are invited to the wedding supper of the Lamb!"'* On this occasion, a union is celebrated too. In the NT the church is pictured as the bride of Christ, those he purchased at the cross. Here at the table of the final wedding supper, Christ is sitting with his own, and turns to the Father who lost us once before, and says, "Father, your family. They've come home."

9
The Invitation

One morning, at about the age of nine, my parents called me into their bedroom. My first thought was that I'd done something I shouldn't have, and the time of reckoning had come. My father was holding an envelope with very colourful edges, from my Aunt Kathleen in New York. Several months previously, she had successfully applied to become a nurse in that city. It seems that although she loved the work she had become very homesick and was inviting me to come and stay with her for the summer.

When my Dad asked if I wanted to go, I was speechless. I couldn't wait to tell all my friends at school. To be honest, not all believed me; this was the world of Kojak and other tv characters, not 9-year-olds from back-street Belfast! Before long my mum and I were out buying all the necessary items: sun cream, swimming shorts, new underwear, etc. I was counting down the days until it finally arrived.

After all the embarrassing, emotional ritual at the airport, a stewardess took charge and promised to look after me during the flight. The Pan-Am 707 was amazing. However, one incident blew all the bulbs on my amaz-ometer During the flight, just after perusing the inflight magazine and looking at clouds had lost its edge, the stewardess asked me if there was anything I'd like to do. Now, she probably felt quite safe as there was a limit to what was possible. I decided I'd ask if I could go up into the cockpit and meet the Captain! Half an hour passed; I thought she'd forgotten me or hoped

I'd forgotten her! She returned, and to my utter amazement, took me by the hand into the cockpit, where, the co-pilot had left his seat, your's truly was invited to sit in it. I sat there for at least a half-hour. I even held the half steering wheel thingy in front of me. I ate breakfast cereal with the Captain, out of a strange-sized carton into which the stewardess poured milk!

Now, if you're wondering where is this going? Let me ask: how many of the children, back at school later, do you think believed that it happened? Another question: do you believe it happened? And if not, what would cause you to believe? What would cause you to believe the NT record of the phenomenon of Christ? A few factors are an encouragement to believe.

First, could it happen?

We might answer, 'Probably not, for these things don't happen today.' That's true, they don't. The horror of 9/11 has made airline cockpits among the least accessible places on the planet. But to argue it didn't happen then because it doesn't seem to happen now is a weak argument. In my case, the conditions, and what that made possible for the characters involved, was different; in the gospel, the character, and therefore what was possible in the conditions, was different. The gospel never pretends Jesus was merely a man, but One who was present at creation and upholds all things by his powerful word; the divine logos (John 1v1-3) who imbued the world with rationality and order.

Remember, wonderful as the laws of nature are, they don't *govern* how the world works, but *describe* how it normally works. Even in science, and with the arrival of 'quantum physics,' exclusively mechanistic, predictable notions of the fundamental nature of reality, have had to give way, at least at the subatomic level. And so, as Banks argues, 'while nature is regular and fixed, it is not logically impossible to conceive of the suspension (not to say violation) of its 'laws' by their creator' (2006, p309).

Secondly, who says it happened?

Could my word be trusted? At the age of 9, that's not a foregone conclusion. My testimony may be tainted by the advantages I had to gain, such as the admiration of my peers. But there is no evidence to suggest that Jesus or his apostles were deceiving anyone. What motive might they have had for doing so? The experience of witnessing to Jesus didn't bring advantage, but terrible cost. From the limited evidence, it seems all except one of the apostles died a martyr's death, rather than confess to fabricating their story. Persisting with the story that Jesus rose from the grave put most of them six feet under.

Thirdly, is there evidence it happened?

We don't find the kind of evidence for Jesus rising again in a test tube; you can't prove it happened in that absolute and scientific sense. But historical evidence doesn't work that way. It proposes likelihood's and probabilities, based on testimonies, texts, citations, inscriptions, and artefacts. The more of these that corroborate the event, the greater the likelihood it happened.

As it happens, very few at school believed I had been in a major airline cockpit, flying over the Atlantic, having breakfast with the Captain. But that conviction weakened when I produced two Pan-Am pen-sets, a Pan-Am leather belt, Pan-Am playing cards, keyring, and a yo-yo! These items didn't prove the event I said had happened, but they helped support its likelihood.

When we turn to the resurrection of Christ, some facts are very hard to explain, unless something of the scale of resurrection happened. Why did those who claimed to

witness it, refuse to deny it, when their life depended on
it? What happened to make a bunch of frightened Jewish
working-class men, who previously denied knowing him,
come out of hiding, and into the town square proclaiming,
"Jesus is alive," unless for them he was? Why did a band of
men, whose life-long, centuries-old defining belief in sabbath
observance, decide Sunday was now more appropriate? It was
because Jesus rose on a Sunday, and so that day, not Saturday,
would never be the same again.

These, and many other considerations, some of which I've
just discussed, are why I believe, and you can too! But there is
another reason, and that's personal experience. In the OT, the
psalmist invites readers to 'taste and see that the Lord is good,'
(Psalm 34v8). In John's gospel, Jesus says, *This is eternal life,
that they (my disciples) may know you, the only true God, and
Jesus Christ whom you have sent,'* (John 17v3).

What is it to know God and Jesus? Well, neither has
appeared to me at the bottom of my bed. I have only heard an
audible voice in prayer, once. I have, however, had countless
promises made to me in Scripture, and found them kept some
of them with an arresting and extraordinary exactness. I've
known what it is to have almost every support in life taken
and still, he has comforted and encouraged me with his felt
presence - I have never been alone. On a few occasions I have
been overwhelmed by the Holy Spirit, as he filled me afresh
with an anointing I will never forget.

All these experiences, however, although grateful
confirmations find their centre in the person of the saviour,
Jesus Christ. The gospel tells us that in him are found the
manifold riches of God's Grace. He, by his death, resurrection
and life at the father's right hand (*the place of power*) has
birthed on planet earth, another way of 'being' that finds its
resource for living, not in ourselves, but in him. As we look
to him, life *(zoe)* happens to us. He stands at our door and

knocks, and promises, "If anyone hears my voice and opens the door, I will come in and eat with that person, and they with me."

A Personal Invitation

If you have been convicted by what you've read and you feel you want to know God, and His Son Jesus Christ - find a Gospel of Mark, or John, and read it.

When you have, you will be left with an impression of their leading character, Jesus. However faint that impression, because you now know he rose from the dead and is alive, close your eyes and address him in prayer. Words along the following lines may help:

Jesus, I am persuaded you are alive. I am also persuaded I need you, and the benefits of both your death and resurrection. Please forgive me my sins, and fill my life with your Spirit. Release me from the destructive behaviours of my past, that separated me from you, and empower me to live the life the Father deserves from me, and I was made to live. Thank you Jesus, my saviour and Lord; Amen.

References

Chapter 1
W. Shakespeare; Hamlet; Act 5, Scene 2
C.S. Lewis; The Problem of Pain; p,3

Chapter 2
Wright, N.T.; The New Testament and the People of God; SPCK; 1992.
Augustine; Confessions; 1.1.1.
Denton, Michael; quoted in: Lennox John, God's Undertaker, Lion, 2009; p.122-133
Flew, Anthony; There is a God; HarperCollins, 2008, Ch.2 'Where the Evidence Leads' & Ch.8 'A Pilgrimage of Reason, p.88'
Spitzer, Robert J.; New Proofs for the Existence of God: Contributions of Contemporary Physics and Philosophy; Eerdmans, 2010; p.65
Davis, P.; God and the New Physics, Simon & Schuster, 1983; p.189.
McGrath, Alister; Mere Apologetics; Baker Books; 2012; p.99.
Lennox, John; Can Science explain everything?; Good Book Club; 2019, p.50.
Collins, F.; The Language of God; Free Press; 2006 - quoted in: Gumble, N.; Questions of Life; Hodder & Stoughton; 2018; p.18.

Chapter 3
Edwards, B & Anderson, C; Through the British Museum with the Bible; 2004; p.55, 63-65; DayOne.
Holland, T; Dominion: The Making of the Modern Mind; Little Brown Books; 2019
Dunn, James D,G; Jesus Remembered; Erdmans; 2003; p.855
Boyd & Eddy; Lord or Legend; Baker Books; 2007, 67

Chapter 4
Keener, C; Gospel of John; 2003, p.552
Troxal, A. Craig; With All Your Heart; Crossway; 2020.

Chapter 6
Packer, JI; God's Words; IVP; 1981; p.153-155.

Chapter 7
Nee, Watchman; The Normal Christian Life; Tyndale (1957, 1977).
Lloyd-Jones, D.M.; Expository Series on Romans, Ch.6 'The New Man.'
Banner of Truth, 1972
Bridges, J; The Discipline of Grace; NavPress; (1994, 2006).

Chapter 8
Beale, G.; A New Testament Biblical Theology; BakerAcademic; 2011; p.678
Packer, J.I.; Keep in Step with the Spirit; IVP 1984, 2005; p.89 Milne, B.; Know the Truth; IVP 1982,1998; p.338.
Beale, G. (with Campbell, D.H.); Revelation; Eerdmans; 2015; p.466 Benyon, G.; Last Things First; IVP; 2010; p.70.
Milne, B.; Heaven and Hell (BST); IVP 2002; p.137.
Grudem, W,; Systematic Theology; IVP 1994; p. 1162.

Chapter 9
Banks, R.; The Gospel of Luke; Colourpoint Educational; 2006; p.309

Further Introductory Reading
Science & Faith
Lennox, J; God's Undertaker; (2009)
Lennox, J; Can Science explain everything; (2019)
Galloway, D.; Noble, A; Follow the Science; Ritchie (2021)

Biblical Text
Williams, P.J; Can We Trust the Gospels; Crossway; (2018)

Jesus and History
Boyd G.A.; Eddy; Lord or Legend: Wrestling with the Jesus Dilemma; (2007)
Is Jesus History; (John Dickson; 2019)

BV - #0023 - 141221 - C0 - 215/143/5 - PB - 9781649601995 - Gloss Lamination